P9-BZT-111

World Mythology
in Bite-Sized Chunks

Mark Daniels

MJF BOOKS
NEW YORK

Published by MJF Books
Fine Communications
322 Eighth Avenue
New York, NY 10001

World Mythology in Bite-Sized Chunks
LC Control Number: 2014937476
ISBN 978-1-60671-255-9

Copyright © 2013 by Michael O'Mara Books Limited

Designed and typeset by www.glensaville.com
Illustrations by Siaron Hughes

This book was previously published as *The Midas Touch*.

This edition is published by MJF Books in arrangement with
Michael O'Mara Books Limited.

All rights reserved. No part of this publication may be reproduced or
transmitted in any form or by any means, electronic or mechanical, including
photocopy, recording, or any information storage and retrieval system,
without the prior written permission of the publisher.

Printed in the United States of America.

MJF Books and the MJF colophon are trademarks of
Fine Creative Media, Inc.

QF   10 9 8 7 6 5 4 3 2 1

CONTENTS

ACKNOWLEDGEMENTS

My sincerest thanks to all at Michael O'Mara Books, especially to my editor Katie Duce, to Glen Saville for his typesetting, to Siaron Hughes for her illustrations and to Leno for his excellent jacket design.

INTRODUCTION

Throughout human existence, we have pondered the fundamental questions of life, death, nature and our relationships with one another. Astonishingly, across the globe and across an inordinately long time span, our solutions to these queries have been identical: the creation of myths.

From vast civilizations to localized societies the world over, each has created a rich catalogue of its own deities, monsters and myths. These tell the stories of our origins, triumphs and disasters, and act as creative tools to communicate life's most important lessons.

The majority of religions and mythologies contain key features that point to some of the very basic questions we have been asking ourselves since our early development as a civilized species: concerns around mortality, birth, astrology and nature as a whole. Often we have looked to nature to inspire stories to explain the inexplicable, creating deities from the sun, the moon, rivers, the sea and mountains. In trying to make sense of the unanswerable, we humans have a tendency to subordinate ourselves to a higher power far beyond our comprehension.

Most theologies try to appease these gods and heroes of our own creation through sacrifice, music, dance, prayer and ceremony. Through this we give ourselves a way to comprehend and gain control over hugely important – yet unpredictable – matters such as health and death, the annual harvest or the swell of the sea. These rituals give each society a set of traditions that helps to forge a community identity and an individual notion of belonging.

Cognitive scientists have likened the divine experience we derive from group recitation of prayer to the swell of emotion felt at a huge sporting event. We thrive on the sense of togetherness and social cohesion that we feel from communal ceremony, the joint chorus of prayer, or the unifying chant of a football stadium – and myths give us reasons to create such shared rituals.

And if we don't have stories, legends and religion upon which to base our rituals, what are we left with? The atheist's life is punctuated by weddings, funerals and naming ceremonies that lack the sense of occasion created by the smells, bells and mumbo jumbo of an ancient religious ceremony steeped in tradition, and thick with allegorical lessons and stories as large and old as the universe.

Moreover, the richly imaginative stories of myths

and legends serve to make the message within them all the more appealing. A mother telling a child to be nice to other children because it's nice to be nice is not likely to elicit much behavioural change. But if the same message is wrapped up in an ancient story, it – illogically – becomes something much more tangible that a child (or adult, for that matter) can relate to: if you aren't nice to other children, the Greek god Zeus, a big bearded man who lives on a mountain and who carries a lightning bolt, will be most disgruntled. A recitation of some thirty examples of the terrible horrors Zeus has inflicted on other naughty children later and even the storyteller has forgotten that all of this was meant to be allegorical.

World Mythology in Bite-Sized Chunks investigates a rich and staggering collection of tales created to help explain the world, taking a roughly chronological peek into some of the most famous and most intriguing stories behind the planet's greatest civilizations. And by the time we're done, you'll be something of a legend yourself.

Chapter 1:

Australian and Maori Mythology

ABORIGINAL AUSTRALIAN MYTHOLOGY

Although colonized by the British just 225 years ago, Australia's indigenous civilization dates back approximately 70,000 years, and the myths within that culture some 10,000 years. Many of the stories were rooted in the geological features that lay nearby to the tribes that told them. Although the myths were not committed to writing during that period, specific local phenomena described in some stories place those myths within that time frame. It is nothing short of a miracle that the same tales have been passed down from generation to generation, and it is purely by word of mouth the stories survive to be told today.

A colossal landmass, indigenous Australia contained an extraordinary array of roughly 400 distinct tribes, with their own unique language and belief systems. As such, cataloguing just one mythology will barely scratch the surface, so we will instead dip into some of the most fascinating stories from across the whole continent.

Dreamtime

Aboriginal Australian mythology references three main realms – human, land and the sacred realm. During the creation of the world, before human life came into being, there existed an era known as Dreamtime. Following creation, Australian Aboriginals believed people lived simultaneously in both the physical world and in Dreamtime, suggesting that in life and in death an element of each of us resides in the eternal Dreamtime. To better understand and influence the current environment, tribes would sing and pray to the Dreamtime incarnation of whichever person, animal, object or other for which they needed help understanding; for example, appealing to the Dreamtime crocodile to help in controlling the real-life version of the same animal.

The legends of Dreamtime are used as aetiological myths and moral lessons, transposing their lessons onto the lives of their storytellers, and, as such, they remain an important part of Aboriginal culture. Covering such a vast expanse of land, it is understandable that the Dreamtime myths vary from one tribe to the next, and so an individual set of myths becomes very much a part of each clan's identity.

Walkabout

The Aboriginal Australians were – and still are – inextricably linked to the land around them. A hugely important part of their civilization is the concept of 'walkabout', a journey undertaken by adolescent boys during which they retrace the ancient pathways of their ancestors. Along the way, these boys stop at preordained sites and perform a series of traditional ceremonies.

The song and ceremony associated with these journeys of seclusion gave rise to the term 'songlines' to describe the pathways the boys walk upon. These routes criss-cross Australia and link sites such as watering holes, caves, landmarks and notable food sources that are of great importance to different tribes. The young man spends up to several months connecting with the land and with his ancestors through their shared ancient ritual; he learns how to live from the earth itself and to reach contentment and peace through solitude.

He returns, one hopes, a man.

The Rainbow Serpent

Despite the staggering array of belief systems across Australia, one character makes more than one appearance: the Rainbow Serpent. The stories – and names – attributed to her vary, but she is generally associated with water, and therefore life itself. In many stories, she ends up devouring people but also bringing traditions and customs to the people of Australia. The Rainbow Serpent is used as a creation story, as well as an explanation for laws, customs and the totemic tribal culture across Australia.

During Dreamtime, at the very dawn of time, as the serpent travelled across the length and breadth of Australia, the markings of her wandering created the valleys, rivers and creeks. Eventually, she called forward the frogs, which emerged from the earth with heavy bellies full of water. The Rainbow Serpent tickled their stomachs and the water poured out across the world, filling the rivers and lakes. From this all other life – both plant and animal – emerged. The kangaroo, emu, snake, birds and other animals then followed the Rainbow Serpent as she moved across the land, with each animal helping to retain the ecological balance by hunting only for its own kind.

The serpent brought in laws and decreed that those who disobeyed them were to remain in their animal form, while those who were well behaved were upgraded to human form. Each tribe was given a totem of the animal from which they came as their identifying icon and to remind them of their origins. They were permitted to eat everything except their ancestral animal, which meant there would be enough food for everyone – a useful tenet in a land where resources are so scarce.

The Sun

In the very early days of Dreamtime, before the sun was created, a young girl, desperately in love, was forbidden from being with her chosen beau. In frustration, she ran away, fleeing deep into the bush, far from food and protection and encountering increasingly harsh conditions. Her tribe in pursuit, the love-struck girl was forced to enter even more inhospitable places.

Upon seeing the young girl asleep and very close to death, the spirits of her ancestors decided it was time to intervene. They lifted her up into the sky, where she woke to find food to eat and fire to keep her warm. She could see that her people were cold and in the dark, and unable to keep their fires going all day long. So even though she missed her family and longed to return to them, she knew she now belonged to the sky and that it was her duty to help her family.

Building her fire as big as she could, the young girl kept it burning all day long so that her people would have warmth. The creation of the sun brought her much happiness, and she resolved to relight it every day to enable her family to go about their business.

The Moon

One fateful day, a great hunter of the Dreamtime era known as Japara left his wife and young son to hunt down his daily catch. In his absence, Parukapoli, a wandering storyteller, happened upon Japara's wife and sat regaling her with wonderful tales in which she found herself completely lost. Her concentration was broken only by the sudden splashing sound of her son crawling into the stream. She rushed over to save him, but it was too late – the young boy had drowned.

Cradling his lifeless body in her arms, she sat there sobbing all day long waiting for Japara's return. When she explained to him what had happened, her husband flew into a rage and blamed her for the death. He took out his weapons and killed his wife, and then he turned on Parukapoli. The two men fought, both sustaining many injuries, but it was Japara who eventually emerged victorious, killing the storyteller.

Berated by his tribe, Japara soon saw the error of his ways. He went in search of the bodies of his wife and son, but soon found they had disappeared. He lamented his actions and pleaded with the spirits that had taken them away that he be reunited with his family. The spirits acquiesced and allowed Japara entrance into the sky world so he could look for his family, adding that, as punishment, he must search the lonely sky for them himself.

It is said that you can still see the scars from Japara's fight with Parukapoli in the lines on the moon, which is itself a reflection of the campfire he lit to help him in his desperate quest to be reunited with his family. The changing route and shape of the moon is an illustration of poor Japara's endless search.

MAORI MYTHOLOGY

The first Maori settlers arrived in New Zealand (or Aotearoa, as it was known) from Polynesia in the thirteenth century AD. The Maori tradition of New Zealand is entirely independent of Aboriginal Australia, and has been grouped within this chapter for reasons of geography.

Maori tradition has a rich polytheistic clan and its myths are deeply entwined with nature. The early Maori people descended from the same Polynesian, Micronesian and Melanesian settlers who had travelled the length and breadth of the Pacific to inhabit islands as far-flung as Hawaii and Fiji. This ancient itinerant history has rendered Maori people in respectful awe of the sea, and may explain why many of their myths contain themes of travel, loss and separation.

Ranginui and Papatuanuku
(Sky Father
and Earth Mother)

According to Maori mythology, Ranginui (abbrev. Rangi), the Sky Father, and Papatuanuku (abbrev. Papa), the Earth Mother, were the progenitors of all earthly things. In the beginning, there was nothing (a theme common to almost all creation myths), and, within this darkness, Rangi and Papa lay embracing one another tightly for millions of years. The fruits of their bond was a brood of all-male children, all of whom were forced to live in the cramped space between their parents with nothing but blackness surrounding them.

As the young men grew bigger, they became increasingly irate at their predicament and began to argue about how they should separate their parents. Tumatauenga, the god of war and the most belligerent of the brothers, wanted to kill both parents, but luckily it was the plan of Tane-mahuta, god of the forest, the brothers opted for: they would prise their parents apart.

Each child tried in vain to separate Rangi and Papa, but to no avail. The onus was once again on Tane-mahuta, who used his enormous strength to pull the earth away from the sky, bringing light and the first dawn into the world. Devastated at this separation, Rangi rained down tears of anguish, which created the rivers and lakes. Each brother found a role as a result of their parents' split: Tawhirimatea, the god of wind, who had wanted to leave things just as they were, found solace in the sky, later beating down all of brother Tane-mahuta's trees with his gusty power; Tangaroa, the god of the sea, fled Tawhirimatea's fury and found protection in the ocean.

Even today, the grief of the couple's separation can be felt: Rangi continues to cry sad tears, which fall to the earth as rain, and his estranged wife Papa unleashes earthquakes in a vain attempt to break up the land, and therefore the distance, that sits between them. But the two remain separated for ever.

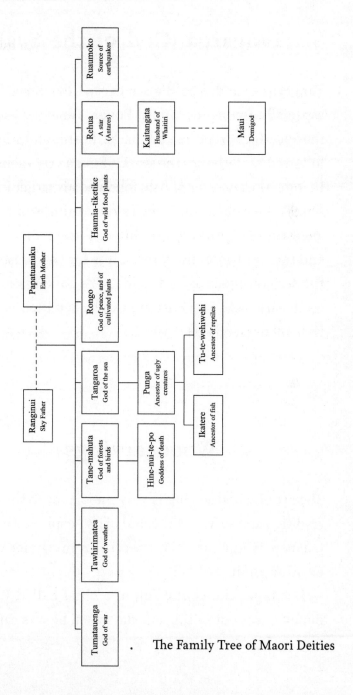

The Family Tree of Maori Deities

Tangaroa (God of the Sea)

Tangaroa's exodus to the sea caused much confusion, especially among his family. Punga, Tangaroa's son and the ancestor of reptiles and sharks, lizards and stingrays, followed his father to the sea. Of Punga's two sons, only Ikatere, the ancestor of fish, followed his father into the sea. Tu-te-wehiwehi, Punga's remaining son and the ancestor of reptiles, found himself stuck on dry land and took refuge in the forests. It is for this reason that the sea continues to be at odds with Tane-mahuta and erodes the land in an attempt to be reunited with his rightful descendants.

Woodcarvings

The art of woodcarving is very important to the Maori tradition and serves as a record of its people and culture. Unsurprisingly, its history within mythology is an exciting affair.

Te Manu, the young son of a chief called Rua-te-pupuke, was out sailing one day when he was captured by Tangaroa. In desperation, Rua went in search of his son. On finding Tangaroa's home, Rua found it covered in intricate woodcarvings, among which he saw his son dangling from the roof, much like a wall hanging. In a fit of rage, Rua was determined to kill Tangaroa, but was advised by Hine-matikotai, an elderly caretaker, to enter the home and fill up all the cracks and crevices to block out any external light. On entering the home, Rua found it bursting with more woodcarvings, all of which, unlike the carvings on the exterior of the house, appeared to be speaking to each other. Rua addressed them and they agreed to carry out his plan.

Written in Ink

The distinctive, intricate designs of Maori woodcarvings are replicated today the world over in 'tribal' tattoos.

The following morning, all was silent. Tangaroa, his son, grandson and all the other fish tried in vain to wake themselves, but were coaxed back to sleep by the darkness. The scene was set for Rua to take his revenge. Standing outside Tangaroa's silent house, Rua set it on fire. Escapees emerged immediately from the burning building, including Kanae (mullet) and Maroro (flying fish), but with many more fish perishing inside. Rua, too, managed to flee the wreckage, picking up a handful of the exterior woodcarvings en route, bringing the non-speaking version of the art form into the human world.

The intricate patterns seen inscribed in wood are said to be inspired by the patterns of fish scales, which could explain why Tangaroa is associated with them. In honour of the killing of Rua's son, it is traditional for Maori homes to have a gargoyle-style boy (known as a tekoteko) on the rooftop of a house as a protection against intruders.

Tumatauenga (God of War)

Tumatauenga was the most belligerent of Rangi and Papa's offspring. He had wanted to kill his parents in order to separate them and let light into the world. Although his brother Tane-mahuta's more sensible plan was accepted, Tumatauenga's fighting talk did not stop there.

Opposed to the actions of his brothers, Tumatauenga created traps to catch the birds (the children of his brother Tane-mahuta), nets to catch the fish (the children of his brother Tangaroa), and created tools to harvest the land – the fruits of his brother Rongo, the god of agriculture. It is for these reasons that Maoris can happily eat animals, fish and vegetation, even if they are the offspring of the gods. The only one of his brothers Tumatauenga could not tame was Tawhirimatea, the god of wind, who continues to this day to express his foul moods through the medium of bad weather.

Tumatauenga is a crucial deity of enormous stature because he has enabled humans to make full use of the land and sea by eating fish and cultivating crops.

Maui-Tikitiki (Demigod)

Several generations down from Rangi, Papa and their characterful offspring was a demigod known as Maui, responsible for many exploits. As a young boy, Maui would watch jealously as his older brothers went out fishing in their canoe and returned with a haul of fish. He would beg every day to be allowed to go with them, but they refused, mocking his youth and size. Not to be deterred, Maui sat down in secret and, using a traditional Maori incantation (a karakia), prayed for his fishing line to be given extra strength.

Maui hid himself in the fishing canoe and his brothers set out to sea. When they were far out, Maui revealed himself – much to the dismay of his siblings – and promised they would catch more fish than ever with him there. As his brothers swung their lines, Maui sang out his karakia and very soon the little canoe was filled with fish. Next, it was Maui's turn. Using his own blood as bait on the hook made from the magical jawbone of his grandmother and chanting his invocations, Maui cast his line, which travelled far down into the world of Tangaroa. When it became taut, it was clear Maui had happened upon a significant catch. Their canoe was dragged from side to side and pulled along by the mighty fish, forcing Maui's brothers to beg him to cut the line. But he held tight and eventually reeled in what can only be described as a *really* big fish.

While his brothers guarded the fish, Maui went back to his people in Hawaiki (the mythical homeland of the Maori people, and from the same linguistic route as the word Hawaii) to get their help in bringing the big fish home. But on their arrival back at the canoe, Maui and his helpers found the greedy brothers hacking away at the fish, claiming parts of it for themselves. Luckily, however, the fish was so enormous that all the people and animals of Hawaiki were able to fit on it. The big fish became the North Island of Aotearoa (New Zealand), and the mountains and valleys are evidence still of the brothers' greedy hacking. Maui's canoe was also inhabited as the country's South Island. Even today, the Maori names for the islands of New Zealand are Te Ika-a-Maui ('the fish of Maui') for the North Island and Te Waka-a-Maui ('the canoe of Maui') for the South Island.

Hine-Nui-Te-Po
(Goddess of Death)

Hine-nui-te-po was the daughter of Tane-mahuta (god of the forest), but he also took her as his wife. When she discovered that he was in fact her father, Hine-nui-te-po fled to the underworld in shame, whereupon she became its ruler.

Despite the many achievements of Maui, which included slowing the course of the sun so that light lasted all day, he lived in the knowledge that he would one day die, following an omen cast over him by his father on the day of his baptism. Not to be cowed by such trivialities, Maui resolved to visit Hine-nui-te-po and trick her into granting him immortality.

Ahead of his visit, Maui gathered together a flock of different birds to take as his companions. He then made his way to the goddess, who could be seen as the red glow on the western horizon. A startling physical presence, Hine-nui-te-po's hair resembled seaweed, her mouth a barracuda and she had eyes of bright-red stone. When Maui and his companions reached her, she was asleep on her back with her legs wide open, in between which they could see sharp shards of volcanic glass and rock.

This was the entrance to the underworld.

Maui gallantly removed his clothes, revealing the intricate fish-scale patterns of his Maori tattoos, and entered in between Hine-nui-te-po's legs with his entire body. Although he had begged his avian friends not to make a stir until they saw him emerge from the goddess's mouth, the absurd scene was too much for one little bird, who let out an excited chirrup of laughter.

Hine-tui-te-po awoke immediately and crushed Maui in two with her razor-sharp vagina and he became the first living thing to die. It is because of Maui's experience that all Maori people must experience death.

Chapter 2:

Sumerian Mythology

Who Were the Sumerians?

Ancient Mesopotamia shown against present-day borders

The Sumerians were an ancient civilization that lived in Sumer, in southern Mesopotamia, from c. 4000 BC. The name 'Mesopotamia' was coined by the Greeks and it referred to the land 'between the rivers' Euphrates and Tigris, in what today is Iraq and Syria. In fact, it was the flash flooding of these rivers that some Christians attribute to the inspiration for the Biblical story of Noah and his ark, and Sumerian mythology itself also contains tales of a destructive flood. Interestingly, geologists have found evidence of several very serious floods in the region from 4000 BC to 2000 BC. Although, it seems that flood myths together with the idea of destruction and cultural rebirth are common: we see similar tales told by the Greeks, the Romans and the indigenous Central Americans (see more on Mayan floods on page 111). And it is of course likely that evidence of floods can be found near most confluences of large rivers.

People settled in the region from the fifth century BC, and communities that were later to become large city-states were founded. Over the following millennium, Semitic people known as the Sumerians migrated in from all sides, including from the Syrian and Arabian deserts, and the region began to flourish. Their glory days lasted until about 2300 BC, making them one of earth's earliest civilizations. However, eventual infighting between the city-states weakened their united power against outside forces. (A common error that has seen the downfall of many civilizations, including the Roman Empire.) The Sumerians were the proud owners of one of the earliest forms of writing, a syllabic alphabet now known as cuneiform, and their knowledge in early astronomy and mythology alike went on to influence many other civilizations, including the Greeks.

In the Very Beginning

The fragments we have of Sumerian text are just that – and so piecing together their stories is tricky at best. Their cuneiform alphabet wasn't deciphered until the nineteenth century, but their texts tell us of the kings (some real, some mythical), gods and cosmology of this ancient civilization.

In one fragment, we can see a start to the creation of the universe that is common to several other belief systems: the separation of the earth and the sky. In the case of the Sumerians, it is the sky god, An, and his female counterpart of the earth, Ki, who are separated by their son, Enlil. He later overthrows his father to become the king of the pantheon of gods.

In another fragment of text, the goddess of the air, Ninlil, is warned against bathing naked in the river, should it attract the unwanted attentions of Enlil. Inevitably, Ninlil blithely finds her way down to the river at the first opportunity, where she is accosted by the enamoured Enlil and impregnated with the moon god Nanna. Appalled by this behaviour, the other deities banish Enlil from the land of the gods, sending him and his pregnant lover towards the underworld.

Enlil seemingly can't bear the thought of his son being consigned to such an eternity, and so devises a plan that, to modern-day audiences, may seem a touch illogical: he disguises himself as three different characters in the underworld – a gatekeeper, the river owner and the ferryman – each of whom impregnates the poor Ninlil. When she gives birth to her various offspring, including the three lesser deities, Nanna is free to ascend to the sky where he belongs, leaving his parents and siblings behind.

A Modern Myth From the Sumerians

The tablet shown here was created from a cylindrical carved stone, which is then rolled over clay to imprint an image. These cylinder seals were used as official stamps and even worn as jewellery by Sumerian dandies, with each cylinder depicting a different scene. The one below pictures a leader of some sort officiating at a ceremony between two people, and it has caught the imagination of many modern-day conspiracy theorists because of the alleged appearance of the sun and planets in the sky.

The Sumerian cylinder seal imprint that implies ancient knowledge of our solar system

In between the two standing characters can be seen what looks to be the sun surrounded by eleven celestial bodies, with a twelfth one further away towards the seated character. Zecharia Sitchin published a book in the 1970s about the significance of this imprint, claiming that the eleven dots resembled the nine planets of our solar system, alongside two of its moons – thus making this an extraordinary example of the Sumerians' knowledge of astrology and their understanding of the solar system many thousands of years ahead of anyone else.

But he didn't stop there. According to Sitchin, the mysterious twelfth dot outside of the 'solar system' represents a planet called Nibiru, from which aliens would come to visit the Sumerians every 3,600 years to experiment on them, teach them things and fornicate with their wives. He states that the myths that tell of the Anunnaki gods coming to the mortal world were in fact these alien excursions and not (as most would believe) just the visits of gods descended from An.

There are a few problems with this theory – most crucially that the Sumerians describe their worldview in texts, which is akin to the idea held by other early civilizations that the earth is flat, underneath which sits a deathly underworld beneath it, and all of which is surrounded by celestial water. No mention is made of the sun and the solar system. Nonetheless, this theory has captivated some people's minds, and the Internet is awash with theories of aliens from 'Planet X' visiting the earth every few millennia, despite the fact that no one thought to record such a visit in the intervening excursion that must have occurred between the Sumerians' heyday and today.

However, this goes to show our general willingness to latch on to myths and believe any story to rationalize the inexplicable. Conspiracy theorizing is just another example of myth-making – a nonreligious approach to creating a higher being that holds the secrets to the world's mysteries.

GODS AND HEROES

The Sumerians created an extensive pantheon of gods. There are many characters in their myths that are cognate with deities in other mythologies – such as gods dedicated to the sky, the earth, the sea, the moon and war.

The fragments of Sumerian texts that we have deciphered tell us of their early founding gods, and depict them as the first kings of their great city-states, from whom their governing families were descended. This helped set their kings on the highest pedestal possible, and was an excellent way to exalt the leaders to the status of semi-divine – after all, who would dare defy one of the gods' great-great-great-grandsons? This tool was also employed by the Romans – see how Augustus used the story of Aeneas to his benefit on page 174.

Enki

The gods inhabited the idyllic land of Dilmun, where all creatures lived in harmony. Nintu, a female deity, asked Enki, one of the most important Sumerian gods, to produce rains. As the god of water, Enki obliged and, possessing a voracious sexual appetite, tried also to woo Nintu. Giving divine significance to marriage, the Sumerian tale states that Nintu did not indulge Enki's passions until he had made an honest woman of her.

Unfortunately, that is where the honesty ended. Nintu was pregnant for nine days before she gave birth to Ninsar (goddess of plants), who was in turn impregnated by her father. Following a mere nine days of pregnancy, Ninsar gave birth to Ninkurra, the goddess of mountains. Not to break with tradition, Enki impregnated Ninkurra, who in turn gave birth to Uttu. He was also able to woo Uttu into sleeping with him, making her the fourth generation to do so.

At the end of her tether, Nintu removed the latest 'seed' from Uttu's body and planted it in the ground, from which grew eight plants. Not content with having caused enough mischief, Enki decided the plants looked delicious and promptly ate them. But, lacking the necessary body parts to give birth to these offspring,

Enki became sick and experienced swelling in eight places around his body.

Nintu eventually came to his rescue, extracting his semen and giving birth to the eight goddesses herself. Each of these goddesses is associated with the healing of the eight different body parts that were affected in Enki: the mouth, the jaw, the ribs, and so on. The myth acts as an important lesson in the follies of excess, as well as explaining the growth of life (both plant and human) and providing deities to pray to for a variety of ailments.

Gilgamesh and the Flood

The story of Gilgamesh is possibly the oldest story ever to have been written down, so it certainly deserves retelling. Gilgamesh was a king of the ancient city of Uruk in c. 2500 BC, and, from the many different fragments of tablets that tell of his story, we have been able to piece together the legends that surround him. He was said to be a mortal descended from the gods – rich, powerful, beautiful and absurdly strong, but with that came greed, arrogance and a voracious sexual appetite.

The gods sent him an adversary in the form of Enkidu to fight him while he was engaged in a sexual assault – but the plan backfired as the two eventually became firm friends. Finally, Gilgamesh had found a partner in crime who was also a demigod, and just as willing to cause havoc. The gods had to intervene once more when the two overstepped the mark by felling some sacred trees and slaying a cherished bull sent by Ishtar (goddess of love) who had been jilted by the handsome Gilgamesh. The gods decreed that Endiku should be afflicted by a ghastly disease that would lead to death, leaving Gilgamesh to reflect on the possibility of his own death. He then set out on a mission to find out the secret to gaining immortality.

Following all manner of adventures too numerous to detail, Gilgamesh eventually encountered Utnapishtim – a man who had been granted immortality by the gods – and listened avidly to his story. Utnapishtim told how the council of gods had decided that, having tired of the human race, they would command a great flood to kill everyone and start all over again. Only Utnapishtim was told of the imminent flood in a dream by Ea, the god of wisdom, who instructed him to build a huge wooden boat to carry his family and all the animals and plants to safety. When the flood arrived, everyone but Utnapishtim and his menagerie of animals was washed away. After a few weeks at sea, Utnapishtim let loose three birds, the last of which finally signalled to his master that there was land nearby and they had therefore reached safety.

Enthralled by this story, Gilgamesh contented himself with the knowledge that his individual mortality was bearable since that of mankind as a whole was immortal. He returned to Uruk mortal, but certainly happier, and satisfied that his legacy would live on for ever – as has been borne out by the retelling of his story here.

CHAPTER 3:

EGYPTIAN
MYTHOLOGY

WHO WERE THE EGYPTIANS?

The Ancient Egyptians unified as a single civilization along the banks of the life-bringing River Nile in *c.* 3150 BC. The mythical King Meni was charged with unifying what is now known as Upper and Lower Egypt almost overnight, but the truth is it took much longer for diplomatic developments to reach conclusion – but myth, as ever, prefers the simpler route. As the keen-eyed reader will note, this made the ancient Egyptians contemporaries of the nearby Sumerians (see Chapter 2).

We can all of us conjure up an image of Ancient Egypt: mummified dead, pyramids, hieroglyphics, pharaohs and the Sphinx, which illustrates how deeply embedded Egyptian culture was with ritual, religion, myth and a wonderfully unique identity. The Egyptian land and culture reached its peak from *c.* 1500 to 1000 BC, and it is during this time that the divine Pharaohs (about whom we learnt at school) ruled – Hatshepsut, Ramesses the Great and Tutenkhamun, to name but a few.

In the fourth century BC, Alexander III of Macedon, better known as the Greek leader Alexander the Great, conquered the enormous Persian Empire, commandeering a vast swathe of territories that included Syria and Egypt. Over the next eight years, the leader of the Greeks would go on to create an empire that straddled three continents. In Egypt, Alexander founded Alexandria, a new capital city, which still bears the same name to this day. But even in the face of such defeat, the religion and myths of the Ancient Egyptians were barely disturbed and there followed an exchange of wisdom and science between the Greeks and the Egyptians, with Alexandria heralded as a famous seat of learning.

Egyptian mythology was complex, influenced not only by the country's geography, with the Nile at its heart and surrounded by the sea, mountains and desert, but also by its longevity as a civilization. Eighteen successive royal dynasties spanning an extraordinary 2,500 years influenced heavily the culture and religious attitude of ancient Egypt. And for the Egyptians, myths were more than just stories. While the ancient tales of the Egyptian gods had their root in the few certainties of the universe – such as the passage of the sun, moon and stars – they also sought to help with lessons of morality and conduct in contemporary society.

The Creation of
the Universe

There is more than one account of Egyptian creation because, it seems, the different regions that made up the culture each wanted to impose their local deities and aetiological legends on to the ancient stories, and so the names and details vary depending on the story. (The Egyptians later reconciled this with a relenting acknowledgement that inventing the whole universe probably took the work of a number of different deities, all of whom, coincidentally, decided to do so on the same day.)

In the beginning (of one story, at least), there was nothing but a nebulous chaos of nothingness, personified by the god Nun. From this emptiness emerged a pyramidal mound known as Ben-Ben, upon which the creator Atum emerged from a lotus flower, bringing with him light. (It is for this reason that Atum is also closely associated with the sun god Ra.) Atum produced the first generation of gods by masturbating into the void and bringing forth Shu, the god of air, and Tefnut, the goddess of rain and moisture. These two gods in turn procreated, giving birth to Geb, the god of the earth, and Nut, the goddess of the sky, with father Shu lifting up his daughter so she could arch over her brother Geb as a canopy of stars.

Following the creation of the earth, sky and the air between it, Atum ruled over the Egyptian universe as the first ever pharaoh. And, having caught wind of a prophecy that the goddess of the sky, Nut, would give birth to a child that would overthrow him, Atum forbade her from doing so. Unfortunately, Nut failed to oblige and she gave birth to four children: Osiris, Isis, Set and Nephthys – the first of whom grew up to fulfil the prophecy. (The Greeks had a very similar myth in Cronos' struggle for power – see page 144.)

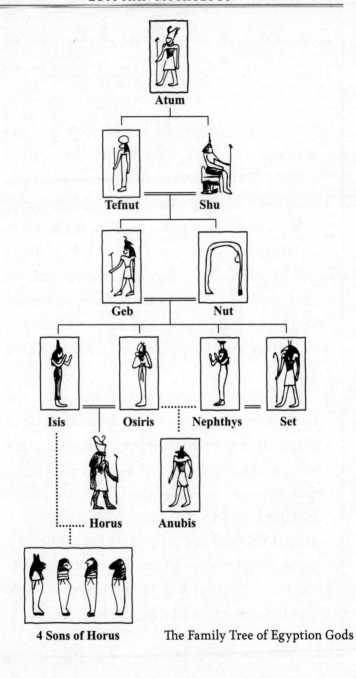

Atum

Tefnut **Shu**

Geb **Nut**

Isis **Osiris** **Nephthys** **Set**

Horus **Anubis**

4 Sons of Horus   The Family Tree of Egyption Gods

Heart vs Ma'at

When Atum created the world, the chaos and disorder of Nun was pushed out to beyond the borders of the universe. In its place was left a wonderful sense of balance, justice and cosmic harmony, known as Ma'at. This principle of universal truth was present in all elements of Egyptian life, informing their morality, their understanding of cosmology, as well as their laws and politics. The personification of Ma'at was a young goddess, often seen wearing a feather.

Egyptians thought the soul resides in the heart. When an Egyptian died, Anubis (god of the dead) would take their heart and place it on a set of scales, weighing it against Ma'at's feather. The outcome determined how closely the person had lived their life according to Ma'at principles. Hearts that did not make the grade suffered a second death and were consumed by the goddess Ammit – a hungry hybrid of lioness, crocodile and hippopotamus (the most frightening man-eating creatures known to the Egyptians) – and their bodies were condemned to an eternity in the underworld, known as Duat. Those whose hearts balanced on the scales with Ma'at's feather faced a far more pleasant outcome: they were sent on to everlasting paradise in Aaru.

The Pharaohs that ruled Egypt were said to be of direct lineage from the gods, and their key role in leadership was thus to uphold the principles of Ma'at. One way to maintain the cosmic balance was through rituals, myth and ceremony in the name of the gods and the Pharaohs – and so it was for this constant affirmation of Ma'at that the Egyptians created such a rich compendium of customs.

The Resurrection
of Osiris

Osiris, who from birth was destined to overthrow Atum to become the ruler of the Egyptian universe, hailed from a close-knit family. He united with his sister Isis, while his brother, Set, formed a union with their other sister Nephthys. However, not content with just one sisterly union, Osiris also embarked on a dalliance with his other sister (and sister-in-law), Nephthys, the result of which was Anubis, the embalming god of the dead.

Angry at this breach of trust, Set jealously murdered his brother, which came to represent the constant struggle between order and disorder under the Egyptian principle of Ma'at. The exact details of the murder are sparsely recorded as the Egyptians gave great significance to their hieroglyphic writing and thought it capable of bringing to reality any destructive things that were written down.

Isis and Nephthys went in search of Osiris' body, and Isis' tears of grief as she searched in vain for her husband and brother gave rise to the idea that they caused the flooding of the Nile each year (and which is why Osiris is seen as bringing life and fertility to the region). With the help of Anubis (funerary god), Isis and Nephthys recovered their brother's body and embalmed it to bring him back to life – a custom that was repeated on the dead throughout Ancient Egypt, with the hope of halting and even turning back the decomposition of the body after death.

However, Osiris' resurrection was only partial, since his subsequent role was as leader of the dead in Anubis' place. Granted only a few moments of life, Osiris took it as an opportunity to procreate with his wife Isis, which bored them a son, Horus.

Horus

The falcon-headed Horus was god of the sky, seen as a protector and a symbol of power, as well as the god of hunting and war. One of the most enduring symbols of Egyptian mythology is the Eye of Horus, which was used as an emblem for protection and guidance in jewellery and sculpture, as well as painted onto the bows of ships. Horus' eyes were said to resemble the sun (personified in the sun god Ra) and the moon (personified in the moon god Thoth). All-seeing eyes are important symbols not only for the Egyptians; similar icons are present in the Christian Eye of Providence, on the back of the US dollar bill and – of course – in the Eye of Sauron in *The Lord of the Rings*.

The Eye of Horus

Following Set's murder of Osiris, he and Horus engaged in an ongoing struggle for power, and a variety of myths tell of the numerous fights, challenges and trickery that ensued between the two gods. One such story sees Horus take a testicle from Set. Another witnesses Set gouging out one of Horus' eyes. In yet another myth, Set tries to impregnate Horus with his 'seed' – considered by the Egyptians to be both a potent poison and a degrading abuse of power. Horus is able to catch the semen in his hands and throw it into the river, and wreaks revenge when he plants his own semen onto a lettuce leaf that Set then eats, thus ending in his defeat.

Despite the violent nature of these stories, they fulfilled an allegorical role. Set is often seen as the god of Upper Egypt (towards the source of the Nile), and Horus the god of Lower Egypt (around the Nile Delta) and their conflict represents not only the struggle between order and disorder to maintain the all-important Ma'at (see page 58), but also the unification of these two lands in the late fourth millennium BC into one country.

Lower Egypt, which includes the fertile and life-giving Nile Delta (and today the cities of Cairo and Alexandria), was dominant over Upper Egypt when the two regions merged into one, and the removal of one of Set's testicles gave rise to the reason why the region of Upper Egypt remained a dry and unfertile desert. The gouging out and later restoration of Horus' left eye (associated with the moon) explains why the night sky goes dark once every month before the moon returns to its visible orbit.

The Wonders of the Ancient World

The oldest-surviving pyramid-shaped structure dates back to around 2600 BC, and ancient Egypt seems to have been littered with such edifices, with well over 100 uncovered by archaeologists to date. The pharaohs of Egypt were considered direct descendants of the gods, and indeed as Horus in human form, and as such were given due pomp and ceremony in their death. Their bodies were embalmed in the belief that this would reverse the decomposition process, and they were buried inside the stone pyramids.

The shape of the structures offered steps up to the heavens, and were originally clad in brilliant polished limestone casing stones, giving them a bright white reflective shine that must have been phenomenal to behold. Their shape was said to mimic that of Ben-Ben, the original mound of the Egyptian universe, from which everything else was created (see page 55).

In some pyramids, the bodies were buried below ground level with all manner of riches, and, in the case of the Great Pyramid at Giza, the artefacts include an entire wooden boat stored in pieces alongside the dead. This largest and most famous of all the pyramids once stood at an incredible 146 metres tall (the equivalent of a forty-four-storey building). Its secret chambers are still being discovered today, and the deliberately perplexing corridors within the pyramids have given rise to the captivating mysticism of Ancient Egypt.

CHAPTER 4:

CHINESE MYTHOLOGY

ANCIENT CHINA

As an ancient culture, Chinese mythology has been influenced by many religious and cultural belief systems. The stories of Chinese mythology have been around for thousands of years and they tell of the beginnings of the Chinese people, of their legendary leaders, and of the bringing of customs and religion. The earliest examples of Chinese writing still in existence are carved onto bone fragments that date back to *c.* 1200 BC. However, it is estimated that the earliest ruling dynasty emerged approximately one thousand years before this from 2100 BC, when the Xia dynasty is thought to have ruled along the Yellow River valley, which means the stories and beliefs that define this civilization would have arisen from as early as this time.

From around 485 BC, China was divided into several competing states, out of which rose the Qin dynasty in 221 BC, which formed China's first united empire. Although the Qin dynasty lasted until only 207 BC, it established the approximate boundaries and basic administrative systems that are still a feature of modern-day China. And from such early beginnings, China has grown to become the largest country in the world – with one-fifth of the world's population and a staggering 1.3 billion people falling under its jurisdiction.

Bai She Zhuan
(The White Snake Woman)

The legend of the white snake woman, which tells of the spirits of a white snake and a green snake, who live in the West Lake of Hangzhou, has been in existence for hundreds of years. It has been the subject of many Chinese plays, novels, operas and, even, movies and computer games, and, as such, many different versions of it are told.

The white snake, now known as Bai She Zhuan, and the green snake, known as Xiaoqing, practised Taoist magic in a quest for immortality, and eventually possessed enough power to transform themselves into beautiful women. Bai She Zhuan then met a young man called Xu Xian by the broken bridge of the lake and the two fell in love after he offered her an umbrella in the rain; they eventually married and opened up a pharmacy in a nearby town. But Xu Xian later met a Buddhist monk called Fa Hai, who could sense Xu Xian's new bride was in fact a snake, and he warned him against her. During an annual Dragon Boat Festival, Fa Hai then tricked Xu Xian into giving his wife some arsenic. Pregnant with her first child, Bai She Zhuan's magical powers were weakened, and she could not help but reveal her true form as a white snake. Xu Xian promptly dropped down dead with shock.

Revived with a special herb, Xu Xian's luck quickly came to an end when he was forcibly separated from his wife by Fa Hai and locked in a temple. Bai She Zhuan attempted to rescue her imprisoned husband by flooding the temple in the hope it would flush out Fa Hai. A struggle ensued, but the green snake, Xiaoqing, came to the rescue and helped Bai She Zhuan and Xu Xian to overcome their adversary. The lovers were temporarily reunited at the broken bridge, until Bai She Zhuan gave birth to their son, after which she was captured by Fa Hai and imprisoned in the Lei Feng Pagoda.

Many years later, the green snake returned to free Bai She Zhuan from her jail, by which point her son had grown up to become a Chinese civil servant. The end of the story varies, but one version sees Bai She Zhuan granted immortality but eternal separation from her husband and son, and her spirit can still be seen, apparently, on the long, low broken bridge when it is covered in snow.

Analyses of this story vary according to which adaptation you read, but the idea behind this particular version is the triumph of social morality over individual desire. It was deemed improper for the snake and the young man to fall in love, and it was against the will of the wise monk, hence their punishment. Conversely, the behaviour of the couple that was deemed proper is celebrated: they work hard on a noble business, their son gets a good education and remains loyal to his father. And it is only once their son has achieved social success that Bai She Zhuan is freed from her prison to return to the west lake.

Kua Fu

Kua Fu was the leader of a group of giants, and his story is one of the oldest Chinese fables. It acts as an aetilogical tale for the origins of a variety of geological features, as well as teaching us the importance of humility.

During one particularly hot summer, when the land was parched and the forest was scorched, the giants found themselves too exhausted to move. In an effort to cool things down, Kua Fu vowed that he would chase the sun along its course to capture and tame it. He ran as fast as he could across the land for nine days and nine nights and as he went he brushed off the dust from his sandals, which then formed the large hills on the landscape. He also created three huge mountains from the three stones that held his cooking pot at night.

When Kua Fu finally caught up with the sun, its heat was too much to bear, so he ran to the Yellow River to try in vain to quench his thirst. Still parched, he drank instead from the Wei River – but this failed too to satisfy his thirst. In a desperate final attempt to succeed, Kua Fu headed for the Great Lake – but alas, it was all too much for him and he dropped dead gasping for water.

His story serves to remind us of the importance of leadership, but acts as a very clear warning of the dangers of arrogance. Interestingly, the hero who becomes weaker the closer he gets to the sun can also be seen in the Greek myth of Icarus (see page 166).

ANIMALS AND CREATURES

L ike the other stories examined in this book, monsters and other creatures play an important part in Chinese mythology.

Dragons

One of the most recognizable Chinese symbols is the dragon, seen variously today in the long, snaking puppet of Chinese festivals, in the designs of many Chinese-inspired buildings around the globe, and, of course, in the names of many of our favourite Chinese restaurants. Far from the fire-breathing maiden-snatcher of British legend, the Chinese dragon is a benevolent and auspicious creature, whose graceful flight and magical abilities make it a revered augur of prosperity. It is a hybrid of several animals (a tiger's paws, the eyes of a hare, the horns of a stag, the scales of a carp, and so on), all of which results in a creature that is said to be a sign of great power and prosperity. Ancient leaders would even associate themselves with the dragon to show their authority.

Despite the Western association of dragons with fire breathing, Chinese dragons are associated with moisture, rain and clouds. Their breath is said to produce clouds, their swirling flight to generate storms, and their wrath can bring both floods and drought, depending on their whim. They are the guardians of the weather, the seasons, and even of the passing of night and day.

In art, scultpture and ornaments, the Chinese dragon is often seen clutching or reaching out for a pearl. This represents a very enigmatic truth or wisdom that the dragon is striving for; it symbolizes the very energy (or chi) that brings all things into balance and the universal progenitor of all things. Sometimes the ball is even depicted as the globe itself.

Chinese
New Year

More than just a celebration of the passing of time, Chinese New Year also commemorates a powerful mythological story.

In ancient times, Nian ('the year') was a ghastly monster who indulged his passion for eating people every New Year's Eve. And so, each New Year the people would flee their villages and go into hiding into the mountains until the marauding beast had gone.

One year, an old beggar came ambling into a village just as the inhabitants were making their annual flight. He pleaded with one old woman to let him stay in her home for the evening. She explained their yearly horror, and advised him strongly to join them in the mountains. But he was not to be moved; he swore that in exchange for one night's accommodation, he would fight off the hungry Nian.

When finally, at midnight, Nian entered the village in search of his next meal, he was startled by what he saw. In front of him, the old woman's house was daubed in red paint and surrounded by burning fires and the air was ringing out with the crash and bag of exploding firecrackers. At that moment, the front door of the old woman's house flung open to reveal the old beggar dressed in a red robe and surrounded by the bright lights of his fires. Alarmed by this spectacle, Nian fled the village in fear.

Even today, the people of Chia stay up all night on New Year's Eve to light fires, set off fireworks and decorate their homes in red to ward off the terrible beast.

The Chinese Zodiac

Like many other cultures, the ancient Chinese people associated certain astrological phenomena different aspects of an individual's personality. Each year of the Chinese calendar was linked to a different animal, twelve in total, each of whom possessed its own characteristics that are then transferred onto the people born in that year. The same animals were also used to denote the time of the day (in twelve two-hour chunks).

1936, 1948, 1960, 1972, 1984, 1996, 2008

Rat people are quick-witted, popular and funny. They are very loyal and up for a challenge, but can be motivated by money and greed.

1937, 1949, 1961,1973, 1985, 1997, 2009

Ox people are dependable, strong-willed and good leaders. They are prone to stubbornness and can sometimes feel isolated.

1938, 1950, 1962, 1974, 1986, 1998, 2010

Tiger people are calm and authoritative leaders. They are ambitious, courageous and philosophical, but can be moody and intense, too. Watch out for the claws.

1939, 1951, 1963, 1975, 1987, 1999, 2011

Rabbit people are homebodies who like to be surrounded by family and friends. They are genuine in personality, very trustworthy and will avoid conflict at all costs – which may make them easy prey.

1940, 1952, 1964, 1976, 1988, 2000, 2012

Dragon people are very lucky – this is one of the most powerful Chinese signs. They are natural leaders and have bags of personality, but will do anything to get to the top.

1941, 1953, 1965, 1977, 1989, 2001, 2013

Snake people are an intelligent bunch. They are good with money, seductive and charming. They may be prone to jealousy and have a slightly dangerous edge.

1942, 1954, 1966, 1978, 1990, 2002, 2014

Horse people are hard-working self-starters who are charming but impatient. They love to travel, but this can also come across as being transient.

1943, 1955, 1967, 1979, 1991, 2003, 2015

Goat people are creative beings. Their mind can wander off into its own little world – making them great thinkers and philosophers, but also disposed to anxieties and insecurities and in need of reassurance.

1944, 1956, 1968, 1980, 1992, 2004, 2016

Monkey people are energetic and lively. They are good listeners, but live in the moment and look after their own interests first. They are fun to be around, but may struggle with long-term commitment.

1945, 1957, 1969, 1981, 1993, 2005, 2017

Rooster people are straightforward, practical and think deeply. They are perfectionists and hard-working, which may sometimes come across as being a bit too neat and tidy.

1946, 1958, 1970, 1982, 1994, 2006, 2018

Dog people are trustworthy and honest. They do well in business, but aren't shy of telling the odd lie or having the occasional mood swing.

1947, 1959, 1971, 1983, 1995, 2007, 2019

Pig people are great companions, and enjoy helping others. They have impeccable taste and are inquisitive. They always get a job done and are intelligent. But don't test them – they will react.

CHAPTER 5:

AMERICAN
INDIAN
MYTHOLOGY

WHO WERE THE AMERICAN INDIANS?

The date of the first human migrations to North America is a hotly debated topic, but the continent has been inhabited from at least 10,000 BC, if not very much longer before that. These new inhabitants spread themselves across both North and South America over time, with different civilizations flourishing at different times. The emergence of a culture that we would now associate with American Indians can be seen in the northern continent between around 1000 BC and AD 1000, the later date by which the Mississippian culture had developed the huge city of Cahokia. Situated in what is modern-day St Louis, Missouri, Cahokia reached a population of up to 20,000 people – matching its contemporary London in size.

American Indian culture is centred on a deep spiritual balance with nature, and is intrinsically linked with the land. Animals play a huge part in their mythology: all living things are seen to possess an individual spirit, as well as belonging to the collective spirit of the world. They view their land as belonging to all creatures, and hunters would thank the spirits of the animals they killed for food.

European explorers arrived in America from 1492 onwards, bringing with them, amongst other gifts, disease and colonialism – neither of which made for favourable living conditions. The population of American Indians nosedived in the centuries that followed, in a cultural clash that is still fraught today.

SPIRITS AND RITUALS

The creation myths of the American Indians are as varied as the number of tribes that populated North America. At the point of the arrival of Europeans in 1492, there could have been ten million people or more inhabiting the area that is now the USA, forming over 500 distinct tribal groups. With such figures it is possible to see how diverse the different philosophies could be across one continent.

Wakan Tanka and the Creation

Despite these discrepancies, the Sioux and Lakota tribes shared similar belief systems and customs, which focused on an entity known as Wakan Tanka, which is sometimes translated as 'the Great Mystery' or 'the Great Spirit', and which resembles the universal spirit in all things. It is thought that in the time before anything existed, Wakan Tanka was in a nebulous dark void called Han. The first entity came in the form of Inyan, the rock, who poured out his energy in the form of the blue blood of the seas and created the earth goddess Maka from himself.

In creating Maka, Inyan had given her the elements of discord and negativity (among other things, of course). As such, she started to complain, her biggest gripe being that she was created from Inyan and was not, therefore, her own entity. She was also upset that she was still living in the darkness of Han and so was unable to see a reflection of herself. The third god was Skan, the sky god. Being more spirit than the physical Inyan and Maka, he assumed a much more divine role. He acted as a judge of all things, and so listened to Maka's concerns.

To placate her, Skan decreed that Han should be split in two, dividing her between the upper world, where she was personified as Anp and would exist in light, and below the earth as Han, where she would continue to live in darkness.

In the upper world, Maka saw how beautiful the blue oceans were and how bare she looked, so she took some of the water and wore lakes and rivers as trinkets to make herself feel pretty. Not content, Maka continued to complain, which resulted in Skan creating the fourth primordial god, Wi, whom he placed in the sky to shine light over the earth. He declared that Wi should provide heat, and should cast shadows on all things – which was thought to represent the inseparable individual spirits of all entities – and instructed Anp and Han to share the sky as night and day.

The Importance
of Circles

For many American Indians, the circle represents the most sacred of shapes as it is present in all things, both literally and metaphorically, and prevalent in a variety of rituals. From the dome of the sky and the shape of the earth – it is possible to see circles in everything.

As such, circles are significance in American Indian customs, and huge circular stone structures can be seen lain on the ground across the USA for use during ceremonies. These 'medicine circles' consist of a central stone from which four small lines of stones point out in the opposite directions of the compass. Each line of stones is associated with different colours, elements, animals and life stage. (The Aztecs also associated the four directions with colours and their gods were made up of different-coloured elements, each of which was associated with a particular direction.)

The Sun Dance and
the Ghost Dance

Performed in the summer to provide a successful bison hunt and to replenish the animal population for the future, the sun dance ritual was an annual ceremony steeped in spiritual significance. During the ceremony, the men of the tribe sat in a specially built structure which had an opening to the sky and a tall tree in its centre, upon which was placed a bison skull.

The young men would paint their bodies yellow, wear decorative feathers and take part in several days of fasting, self-harm and ritual, with the intention of becoming unconscious to receive spiritual visitations. The ceremony would culminate with the men attaching cords from the top of the pole to their nipples and performing a dance.

Such activities did not sit well with the Christian sensibilities of white Americans, and the practice was forcibly suppressed. However, it did not die out entirely and soon took on another form as the ghost dance. Popularized in 1889 by an American Indian prophet known as Wovoka, the dance was said to bring the participants closer to the spirits of the dead. In a time when the clash between old and new America was reaching its peak, the dance was carried out to bring unity and balance back to the land and to return the continent to its pre-invasion status.

However, the widespread practice of the dance had the opposite effect. The US military arrested and even killed American Indian leaders who failed to prevent their tribes from performing it – and one attack on a camp in Wounded Knee Creek, South Dakota in 1890 ended in the massacre of more than 150 American Indians. The dead included many women and children, and they were buried unceremoniously in a mass grave.

American Indian Words in Modern Culture

Approximately half the states that make up the USA are named after Native American words or tribes from that region. There are also many everyday words in modern English that have their roots in the languages spoken across the pre-Columbian Americas (north and south), including barbecue, hurricane, tomato, potato, cocaine, moose, racoon and toboggan, to name just a few. Beyond these direct translations into English, we have also adopted American Indian terms to use in our own (commercial) culture to evoke some of the heroism and mysticism of their native myths.

It is undeniable that most of the uses of these terms for commercial benefit are a somewhat narrow-sighted attempt to evoke images of manly, outdoorsy warrior-types, and they do not represent the full picture of the hundreds of different tribes that inhabited the continent. It seems we have bought into our own myth of what it is to be a Native American and continue to perpetuate a stereotype.

	What we think it is	What it really is
Apache	A type of Jeep for off-roading with your friends.	A conglomeration of various tribes from the south-west of the United States.
Cherokee	Another type of Jeep. These days more likely to see a supermarket car park than a precipitous dirt track.	A tribe situated in the south-east of the USA.
Chinook	A military helicopter with two rotors.	A group of tribes situated in the Pacific north-west of the USA.
Mohawk	A hairstyle popularized by the punks of 1980s Britain, often dyed.	A tribe from what is now upstate New York. While they did have rather fancy hair, the modern 'Mohawk' style is closer in cut to that of the Pawnee tribe in today's Nebraska.
Pocahontas	A Disney princess. She falls in love with Englishman John Smith and saves him from execution by the American Indians.	In reality, that's just where the story begins. In the early seventeenth century, Pocahontas married another Englishman after the John Smith incident, in what is thought to be the first interracial marriage in America. She converted to Christianity and moved to London as something of a celebrity, where she died at the tender age of twenty-two from a ghastly disease.

	What we think it is	What it really is
Tomahawk	A long-range exploding missile.	The traditional axe with a head made from sharpened flint or antlers. Some ingenious people even carved a hollow out of the handle so the tool could double up as a pipe.
Quahog	The town in Rhode Island made famous by American animation series *Family Guy*.	A round hard-shelled clam found on the Atlantic coast. The name comes from the Narraganset language, and is short for poquauhock (from pohkeni 'dark' + hogki 'shell').
Winnebago	Huge mobile homes for cross-continent road trips and touring rock bands alike.	A tribe now residing in Nebraska.

THE MYTHS OF
THE PLAINS

The plains covered what is now the Midwest and the south of the USA and the mythological stories associated with this area held important lessons for the American Indians.

The White
Buffalo Woman

Several tribes of the plains tell the myth of the White Buffalo Woman, known as Pteskawin. She acts as a bringer of rituals to these tribes – a role personified by many civilizations the world over to give significance to the customs that are continued in the name of spirituality.

In a time when food was scarce, two young hunters left their tribe before dawn in search of prey. They wandered far and yet found no animals that they could bring back to feed their people. After a long search, they reached the top of a hill and looked out across the prairie, where they spotted something bright coming towards them from the horizon – which, as it approached, turned out to be Pteskawin, a beautiful woman wearing a brilliant-white hide. Understandably taken by the beauty of this unexpected apparition, one of the young hunters approached her with amorous intent. His companion could see that she was wakan (or holy), and urged his naive friend to respect her spirituality. But it was too late: as the woman embraced the young man, a cloud enveloped them both and disappeared to reveal nothing but bones lying at her feet.

Now that she had her audience's attention, the woman instructed the remaining hunter to go back to his tribe and instruct the chief to gather all his people under one tepee for her imminent arrival. Obediently, the hunter ran back at once and a huge tepee was built for all the tribe, in which they all waited in respectful anticipation of her dramatic entrance.

Pteskawin entered the tepee, walked around its circumference following the direction of the sun and stood before the chief on the west side. She gave him the sacred chanunpa (smoking pipe), which was carved with symbols representing the earth, the buffalo, the forest and the birds. It acted as the tool for several important rituals for these tribes, and the smoking of it brought tribesmen closer to the spiritual world.

As she left, Pteskawin was seen to turn into a buffalo, bow to the four directions of the earth and disappear into the horizon. Many of the actions described in the myth continue to be important elements of American Indian culture, particularly for the Lakota tribe from where the story originates: the various uses and meanings of the pipe, the communal lodge, the following of the direction of the sun and the historical importance of the buffalo as a resource.

The Wily Coyote

The cartoon coyote of the same name is inspired by an ancient American Indian myth of the Lakota tribe. In the more traditional version, this trickster was wandering across the plains with his friend Iktome, the spider spirit, when they came across a huge rock. Coyote recognized great soul and life in the rock and saw that it was the spirit Iya.

Coyote took off the blanket he was wearing and placed it over the rock to keep it warm, and the two friends continued on their way. Later on, it started to rain and become cold, and the adventurers sought shelter in a damp cave, where Iktome remained warm under his thick hide and Coyote regretting his earlier generosity. Suddenly recalibrating his morality, Coyote determined that an old rock had no need for a blanket and demanded that Iktome go back to retrieve it. After the spider's unsuccessful attempt, it was left to Coyote to go shivering back and yank the hide from the rock's back himself.

Content, the two companions continued on their journey. However, when they came to rest once again in another cave they heard a distant rumble. The noise was getting louder by the minute as it resonated across the plain and echoed in the cave behind them. Suddenly on the horizon they could see the great rock Iya rolling towards them, crushing everything in its path, clearly making his way to Coyote.

Petrified, Wily and Iktome fled. They tried several techniques to outwit Iya – swimming across the river and weaving in and out of the forest – but to no avail: the rock continued to roll at speed towards them. It was only Iktome who was able to outwit the rock by rolling himself into a ball and disappearing down a tiny hole. The poor coyote, on the other hand, was flattened by the rock.

This is another legend that punishes the disregard of sacred things, and is an illustration of spirit that American Indians saw in all creatures and objects of the earth. They had no temples or shrines – the spirituality of their belief system was alive in all things. Moreover, Iya was seen as a storm god, so the story helps to give explanation to the destructive nature of hurricanes, punishing the sins of Coyote (to use Christian terminology). It also gives us an insight into the morality of the tribe that told this tale: it beseeches the listener to keep their generosity genuine and is a reflection of the very fair and unquestioning kind-heartedness with which the Lakota wanted to treat their fellow tribesmen.

CHAPTER 6:

SOUTH AND CENTRAL AMERICAN MYTHOLOGY

THE MAYANS

The Mayans first emerged as a distinct civilization in c.2000 BC and occupied a region in Central America now covered by Guatemala, Belize and parts of southern Mexico, as well as western Honduras and northern El Salvador. They reached their peak in c. AD 250, and eventually waned around AD 900, but their languages, mythologies and culture are still prevalent in the region today.

Much like the Greeks in their heyday (see Chapter 7), Mayan society was structured as a series of independent city-states, each with its own powerful king. They built wonderful temples and palaces, and are credited with having had the only known fully developed writing system in pre-Colombian America.

Mayan culture was thick with art, ceremony and tradition, and they were partial to human sacrifice too. The Mayans also had very advanced abilities in astronomy, mathematics and agriculture.

The End of the World (Or Not)

People the world over became were excited by the ancient Mayan prediction that the world would end on 21 December 2012, reported in news bulletins across the globe with a slightly nervous tongue in cheek. Bugarach, a small mountain village in southern France, was rumoured to be one of the few places where people would be safe, and some people even bought one-way tickets to spend time with the bewildered locals.

The Mayans categorized dates using three different calendars. The Haab was the civil calendar and it counted 365 days in each cycle, with each year broken into nineteen months, each of which consisted of twenty days, except for one month of just five days. The Tzolk'in was the divine calendar that dictated the dates of religious ceremonies; it counted 260 days in each cycle, which were subdivided into twenty sections of thirteen days each. The final calendar was the Long Count, which was an astronomical calendar consisting of approximately 7,885 years in each cycle. At the end of each cycle, the world would end and be reborn.

Over the years, keen conspiracy theorists worked

out that the end of the latest Long Count cycle would fall on 21 December 2012. Although the Mayans did not predict anything too ghastly – it was just the end of one calendar and the beginning of another, much like we experience each 1 January – worry spread that the end of the world was nigh.

Bugarach's association with the debacle was somewhat absurd. What began as spurious Internet-based rumour-mongering naming the village as a safe haven from the impending apocalypse quickly transformed into something much bigger. The region's mayor dared to mention the village's safe-haven status in a council meeting in the years running up to Armageddon, which was soon picked up by local newspapers. Once it was being reported on news networks across the globe, the association was complete.

This story illustrates the sheer power of myths and storytelling. Even those people who joked about the end of the world still had an uneasy look in their eyes, and those who relocated to France (despite never having heard of Mayan theology before) illustrated how far we are still from understanding the world around us – and how readily we will cling to any elaborate story that seeks to make sense of it.

The Mayan Calendar

The World Tree

The concept of a World Tree is a tradition central to many world mythologies (see page 196 for the Norse interpretation). According to the Mayans, the World Tree (Wacah Chan) formed the very basis of the universe, and was anchored in the Mayan people's astrological observations of the Milky Way, which seemed to grow up into the heavens from the horizon. The roots of the World Tree were based deep down in the underworld (Xibalba), its trunk in the middle, mortal, world and its celestial branches stretching out into the heavens. The trunk of the tree was sometimes seen to be formed from reptilian creatures.

The name Wacah Chan means 'erect serpent', and it describes the bright, straight line of the Milky Way as it emerged from the horizon at certain times of the year. The tree reached out in the four directions in the mortal world, and worked as a reassuring visualization for the Mayan people: the sturdy strength of the tree represented the strong core at both the centre of all humans and the centre of each important ritual, stretching out in all directions, connecting all mortals and all gods.

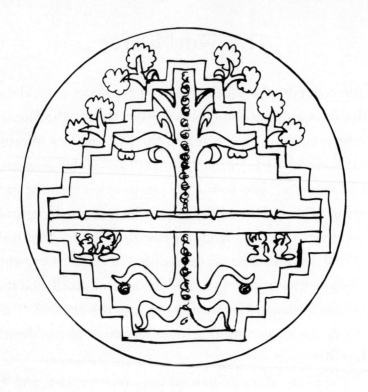

The Mayan World Tree

Itzamná

God of creation, inventor of writing and the calendar, Itzmaná was generous-spirited and married to the rather more mean-natured goddess Ixchel, who filled her palace with vats of water which she would rain down on the worlds below causing huge storms and floods. Itzmaná was the leader of the gods, whom he presided over from his throne, and he became the patron deity of medicine, as well as bringing culture, rituals and knowledge to the Mayan people. Sometimes, he was depicted as four gods (the Itzmanás), each pertaining to one of the four main compass points.

Itzmaná was, according to different sources, either the son of or the visible incarnation of Hanab Ku – the abstract spirit from which everything else came. One myth tells how Hanab Ku created and re-created three sets of mortals in the world before he reached a state of happiness. He destroyed his first creation, the little people, with the help of a water-spewing serpent after he discovered they were not to his liking; his second attempt generated a people known as the Dzolob, whom he too destroyed with a flood after deciding they were not quite right; finally he created the Mayans, by which point he was, thankfully, content.

The physical manifestation of Hanab Ku's spirit in

Itzamná was an elderly man with an enormous hooked nose. He was a benevolent patriarch that protected the Mayan people, who often held ceremonies in his honour at the transition into a new calendar cycle to bring prosperity and health.

Chac

As the god of rain, Chac became an increasingly important figure in Mayan religious ceremonies and human sacrifices. With sharp fangs, huge goggling eyes that shed tears of rain, a snout-like nose, a reptilian body and carrying a serpent axe that represented the lightning bolts for which he was known, Chac cut a distinctive figure. Like the other major Mayan gods, Chac possessed four different personalities, each of which was associated with the four points of a compass, called the Chacs (the name also given to the four priests who would hold down each limb of a sacrificial victim).

In the very beginning of time, Chac split open a sacred rock with his axe, from which sprang the very first ear of corn. He subsequently taught the Mayans agriculture and kept control of water in the atmosphere as well as on the ground, which meant he was held in very high esteem. Chac was associated with frogs, since they signalled the coming of rain, and part of religious ceremonies in his honour would require four young men to impersonate frogs.

The Hero Twins

Hunahpu and Xbalanque were a sprightly set of twins skilled particularly at ball games. So noisy were they about their victories that even the Lords of Death in the underworld (Xibalba) caught wind of their prowess. Having cleanly dispatched of the twins' father and uncle, who had themselves been a boastful pair of ball-playing twins only one generation previously, the Lords were somewhat perturbed by current proceedings. They summoned the boys to the underworld.

The twins were subjected to a similar set of challenges to those their father and uncle had faced. They managed successfully to outsmart the Lords' first trick: having disguised themselves as wooden carvings, the Lords tried to force their guests to sit on a burning bench, but the twins, realizing the seat was hot, refused. The challenges continued. Hunahpu and Xbalanque were handed a flaming torch and cigar each and instructed to keep them burning until the following day. They managed to trick the Lords by tying fireflies to the ends of the cigars and replacing the torch flame with the bright-red tail of a macaw, which gave the illusion that the embers were still burning.

Hunahpu and Xbalanque continued to trick the lords in a succession of further challenges – the most impressive of which saw Hunapu survive decapitation during a ball game by replacing his head with a squash fruit. However, realizing that their luck would no doubt soon run out, the twins accepted one final, fateful invitation from the Lords to step inside a firing furnace, and to their deaths. But the twins were one day able to exact their revenge.

The Lords of Death ground up Hunapu and Xbalanque's bones and sprinkled them into a river, from which they were both reincarnated into several forms. The last of such transformations was two travelling magicians, who were so skilled in their art they could perform human sacrifices and then reverse the process and bring the victims back to life.

The Lords of Death heard of their magical powers and requested a private showing in the depths of the underworld. So impressed by the twins' extraordinary death-reversal abilities, the Lords asked them to perform the trick on some of them. However, the boys, quite understandably, refused to undertake the resurrection part of the trick after they had performed the initial sacrifice. The glory days of Xibalba were brought to a close, and Hunapu and Xbalanque were raised into the sky to take on the forms of the sun and the moon.

THE AZTECS

An itinerant Mexica people united by the Nahuatl language, the Aztecs first occupied the region of central Mexico in the sixth century AD. A turbulent few centuries passed before they finally settled in 1325, when they founded the city of Tenochtitlán, a city-state situated on an island in Lake Texcoco. In 1427, a triple alliance of three Nahua city-states was formed when Tenochtitlán joined forces with Texcoco and Tlacopan, which signified the true unification of an Aztec people. Tenochtitlán acted as the centre of the Aztec Empire until the Spanish conquistadors destroyed it in the sixteenth century. The site of this ancient city is at the heart of where Mexico City stands today.

The itinerant past of the Mexica people gave rise to a mythical fatherland known as Aztlan, from where they had originated (hence the collective noun 'Aztec'), but the site – and existence – of this mythical land has been disputed.

The Aztec
Creation Myth

The Aztecs believed it took several attempts to create the world before getting it right; each failed attempt gave rise to the creation of different creatures. In the beginning was Ometeotl, the very first god of all things. He bore four children, the Tezcatlipocas, each of whom was associated with a point on the compass.

In the first attempt, the earth was inhabited by berry-eating giants. The northern son of Ometeotl was known as the Black Tezcatlipoca, god of discord, light and beauty (among other things). He transformed himself into the sun and looked out over the world. His rival personality in the west was Quetzalcoatl, god of light and wind, who battled with his brother in the north and knocked him out of the sky. In retaliation, Black Tezcatlipoca returned as a jaguar and destroyed the world.

The second attempt at creation came when Quetzalcoatl was ruling the heavens. The people he produced on earth had a fondness for pine nuts, which meant that when Black Tezcatlipoca came down and wreaked yet more revenge when he came as a wind to destroy everything, the few people who were left were turned into monkeys.

In the third attempt, Tlaloc, god of rain, took his turn as the sun, but this time Quetzalcoatl sent down rain that flooded the earth and destroyed everything again. The few people who remained were turned into birds to escape the deluge. Chalchiuhtlicue, the goddess of water, was the fourth one to take on the role of the sun – but her attempts were also destroyed by a flood of her own tears of blood, with the few survivors turning into fish.

Finally, after three failed attempts to create the world, the four gods put their heads together to devise a solution.

Quetzalcoatl resolved to travel to the underworld and retrieve the crushed bones of all who had died, resurrecting them by mixing them with his own blood. According to Aztec mythology, all humans are descended from this fourth and final attempt at creation; the variations in shape and size a consequence of the differences in size of the fragments of bone.

This idea of destruction and rebirth can also be seen in Mayan mythology (see page 106), the Norse concept of Ragnarök (see page 212) and even in Noah's Ark of the Bible.

Tlaloc

Similar to the Mayan god Chac (see page 112), Tlaloc was the Aztec's answer to the god of rain, fertility and agriculture; he was also of a similarly striking appearance, sporting a pair of goggling eyes and protruding fangs. Having occupied such pivotal role in controlling the rain, water and therefore supply of food, temples were erected in Tlaloc's name around the Valley of Mexico. He was also the recipient of notable rituals in his name – including the sacrifice of men and even children.

Be Still
My Beating Heart

Sacrifice was an integral part of Aztec society. Because the gods had sacrificed themselves in the creation of the world, the Aztec people felt indebted to them and offered their own blood as a sign of their subservience. Rituals would sometimes take the form of removing beating hearts from human bodies and offering them to the gods.

Black Tezcatlipoca

THE INCAS

The Empire of the Incas was vast, stretching over 2,400 miles along the Andes in South America. The Incas emerged as a group in *c.* 1200 and reached their height in the fifteenth century, by which point they inhabited a region that covers much of what is now Chile, Peru and Ecuador, as well as parts of Colombia, Bolivia and Argentina. This made them the largest united empire in all of the Americas at the time.

The Inca belief system is centred on the sun, which was seen as the life-giver of all things. As such, it was their ancestral father in the sky, and its importance is reflected in many of their myths. The Incas used their mythology to claim their authority over other tribes.

Unfortunately for the Incas, the onset of the age of discovery in the sixteenth century severely inhibited further growth. Indeed, the European invasion of the Americas didn't bode too well for the longevity of indigenous cultures, and the Incas' turn came around 1526 with the arrival of the first Spanish explorers to the region. Their population was ravaged by disease and war – with the last Inca leader being captured and executed less than fifty years later.

A Familiar
Creation Story

The mythology of the Incas held many similarities with the other indigenous tribes of the region. According to the Inca creation story, in the beginning there was darkness, until the creator god Kon-Tiki Viracocha arose from what is now Lake Titicaca and brought forth the sun god Inti alongside the moon and stars.

As the god of creation, Viracocha – and in scenes reminiscent of both the Mayan and Aztec stories of creation (and not unlike the Christian story of Moses) – was displeased with the first batch of beings on the earth and sent a flood to destroy them all. Some myths tell of these people being turned into monkeys, which is a fate found in Aztec culture, too.

Viracocha created the new human race by scattering pebbles across the land, and bestowed upon them language, clothes, skills and laws, and taught them to develop harmony and knowledge by disguising himself as a beggar and wandering about the land teaching them how to live. According to some accounts of the creation story, Viracocha was dissatisfied still by this second incantation of people and it is thought he will one day return to Earth to redeem the human race or impose upon us another flood.

The Origin of Cuzco

The city of Cuzco lay at the centre of the Inca Empire, situated at 3,4000 meters above sea level in what is now southern Peru. To reinforce the historic importance of this great city, Inca mythology decreed that Cuzco, its location and its rulers were all directly decreed from the gods themselves. (See also the story of Aeneas and Rome on page 174.)

According to one myth, the sun god Inti created the first Incan man and father of the Incas, Manco Capac, and the first Incan woman, Mamaoqlyo, Manco's sister and wife. Inti gave Manco a golden staff, with which he and his sister-wife set off on their task to found the Incan capital. They travelled far and wide across the Andes in search of the sacred site, and knew finally when they had hit the right spot when the golden staff sank into the ground. It was here they built a temple to Inti and taught their people about the sun god from whom they were all descended.

In truth, the city predates the Incas. Before the Incas acquired Cuzco for themselves in the thirteenth century it lay in the hands of the Killke culture, who had occupied the surrounding region since *c.* 900. The city grew quickly under the Incas, but it required a divine myth to give the site prehistoric significance and to exalt the Inca people to godly levels of importance.

The Lost City of Machu Picchu

We cannot explore the Inca civilization without taking a quick trip up the mountains to Machu Picchu, which remains today one of the most iconic images of South America, and one of the most captivating sites of the ancient world. Machu Picchu is a settlement not all that far from the city of Cuzco in modern-day Peru, and the mysticism surrounding its crumbling temples and domestic buildings derives from the fact that it was built some 2,400 metres feet above sea level on a peak in the Andes and lay there completely undiscovered until 1911. Given that it was built in *c.* 1450, and the entire region was the victim of a thorough ransacking by the Spanish explorers from the end of the sixteenth century, it is a wonder that no one discovered this lost site until the twentieth century.

Although theories vary as to the purpose of Machu Picchu – it is thought to have been primarily a sacred retreat built for two of the most powerful Inca leaders, but other theories suggest it housed a population of some 1,000 people across the city – it offers a unique glimpse into Inca life. It houses several distinct areas for sacred buildings, royal palaces, industry, residence and farming. We can see that they had very advanced techniques for step farming up the steep Andean slopes and they used aqueducts to carry water from miles around to irrigate the land.

CHAPTER 7:

GREEK MYTHOLOGY

WHO WERE THE GREEKS?

The civilization of the Ancient Greeks straddled a vast period and brought us, among other contributions, philosophy, literature, drama, theatre, laws, democracy, architecture and Pythagoras' theorem. Excavations in Knossos, Crete, revealed a large palace dating from approximately 2200 BC, which has been suggested as the home of King Minos, the leader of the Minoans. The era of the Mycenaeans followed from about 1600 BC to 1200 BC, and it was events during this period on which most of the epic poems of Homer and the Greek tragedies were based. Thanks to the efforts of Alexander the Great in the fourth century BC, the Greek Empire reached its height, extending all the way across present-day Turkey, Egypt, Israel, Iran and all the way over towards India.

Greek civilization really came into its own in the eighth century BC, when the Greek alphabet as we know it was introduced. The Greeks put their writing skills to immediate good use, committing to paper some of the most famous myths we know today. Homer, the most famous of the Greek poets, lived in eastern Greece at some point between 800 and 700 BC, and his two epic poems *The Iliad* and *The Odyssey* are widely recognized as the first written works in the Western world. Many of Homer's stories still influence books, stories and movies today.

The Greeks were all the rage until they handed the baton (with some resistance) over to the Romans during the second and first centuries BC. But the Romans took so much inspiration from Greek civilization (and which they proceeded to spread across their own empire) that the Greek legacy extended far beyond its own borders. Indeed, Greek mythology can probably lay claim to having had the biggest influence on the modern Western world – we've all heard about the Cyclops, Zeus and Poseidon, to name but three.

GODS AND GODDESSES

The Greek gods were a vengeful and rampant bunch. There were lots of them, too many to mention here, so I've narrowed the focus to the Olympians, who were a group of twelve gods that ruled following the overthrow of the Titans. Eleven of the twelve gods resided on Mount

Olympus; the twelfth god, Hades, was resigned to the underworld. All twelve tended to bicker, argue and fall in and out of love with each other, and they would play out their emotions by meddling with the lives of mortals on earth in order to exact revenge on one another.

Through describing these celestial disagreements and emotions, Greek writers were able to give a bigger context to the reasons behind wars, love and natural disasters.

Zeus

Zeus, the lord of the skies, was in charge of the whole clan, and known as the father of the gods. His elevated status seemed to give him licence to sleep with whomever (or whatever) he pleased. And he had a remarkable ability to turn himself into anything he desired in order to get his way, once transforming into a bull to sleep with Europa, who then gave birth to Minos, King of Crete. As a result of such bedroom feats, an extraordinary number of other deities, demigods and beasts claimed Zeus as their father. In fact, at the last count, a progeny of some 120-plus gods and heroes had been attributed to Zeus.

As with many religions, the daddy of them all was the arbiter of right and wrong. And Zeus seemed a fairly decent fellow when you were on his good side, but he was certainly not someone you'd want to mess with. Zeus is often depicted bearing his trademark thunderbolt, which he'd throw at anyone who had displeased him – something you'd know about if he caught you cheating at poker.

To further complicate matters, Zeus' parents were Cronos and Rhea, and he was married to the very patient Hera (who also happened to be his sister).

The Greek Gods' Family Tree

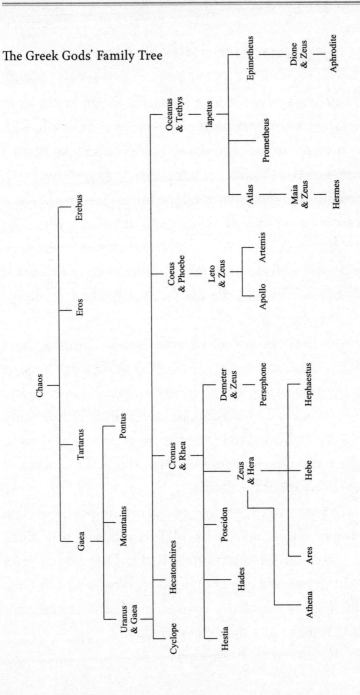

Apollo and Artemis

Apollo was one of the many sons of Zeus, and twin sister of Artemis. In Greek poetry, he represented the sun, with its mysterious passage across the sky being attributed to his chariot pulling it across each day. Conversely, Artemis was represented by the moon. The two of them were born on the hallowed island of Delos – which, to this day, is held sacred, with no one allowed to be born or die on the island. (A far cry from party destination Mykonos, which lies beside Delos and is now in charge of the ancient site.)

Apollo is the god of several things – among them music, truth and healing, as well as being a dab hand at archery. Because of his closeness to Zeus, his astrological importance and his associations with truth, he had many temples dedicated to him – the most famous at Delphi, where the Oracle would channel the god and answer questions about the future.

His sister, Artemis, is the goddess of hunting and wildlife – as well as (contradictorily) childbirth and virginity. There are statues of Artemis from the first and second centuries AD in the ancient city of Ephesus, in what is now Turkey, showing her completely covered in what we assume are bull's testicles as a sign of her fertility.

Poseidon

Poseidon was often an angry sort. As god of the sea, he was known for stomping his trident to create swells, tsunamis and whirlpools. But if you got him on side, he would happily calm the seas and give you a favourable wind.

He was the brother of Zeus and Hades, and the three of them drew straws for shares of the world after they had overthrown their father, Cronos. Zeus and Poseidon lucked out, gaining control of the land and heavens, and the sea, respectively. Poor Hades drew the short straw and got stuck with the underworld, sometimes referred to as Hades in his honour.

Poseidon happened also to be the father of Polyphemus, the King of the Cyclopes and a one-eyed giant made famous in Homer's *Odyssey* – one of the first myths to be committed to writing in the Western world, and still widely told today. In Homer's epic, the hero Odysseus became trapped in a cave by the one-eyed ogre, but managed to outwit him by plying him with wine. When Polyphemus drunkenly asked Odysseus his name, he replied, 'Nobody,' and drove a burning stake through his one eye. When his fellow Cyclopes were unable to find a person by the name of 'Nobody', Odysseus was left free to sail triumphantly away. But, thinking he was safe at sea, Odysseus mistakenly revealed his name to Polyphemus, who duly ran crying to his father, Poseidon, who in turn banished Odysseus to a few more years lost at sea.

Aphrodite

As the goddess of love, desire and beauty, you would expect everything to be peaceful in the world of Aphrodite, but as the wife of Hephaestus, god of fire, and the lover of Ares, the god of war, hers was a hectic existence.

Her beauty is said to have been the catalyst for the ten-year war of Troy that was central to so many Greek myths: the Trojan Horse, Achilles, Odysseus, Aeneas and the start of the city of Rome, to name just a few (more on that in chapter six).

The story goes that, during a banquet held by Zeus, a golden apple inscribed with the words FOR THE MOST BEAUTIFUL WOMAN was thrown into the ceremony by Eris, the goddess of discord. The goddesses Aphrodite, Athena and Hera all claimed the apple for themselves, so it was left to poor mortal Paris, deemed the most eligible bachelor in Troy, to judge who the recipient should be. It wasn't to end well.

The goddesses each undressed and wooed Paris with enticing gifts. But Aphrodite's offer of the hand in marriage to Helen of Troy – the most beautiful mortal in the world – was to prove the most alluring, so Paris gave Aphrodite the golden apple. The trouble was Helen was already married to the Greek king Menelaus, who got a bit annoyed at his wife's infidelities and stormed over to Troy (with hundreds of thousands of Greek soldiers in his wake) to get her back.

Eros

The Greeks had two words for 'love': *agape*, which refers to a kind of deep and soulful love; and *eros*, which refers to more physical desires and needs. It is from this type of love that we get the English word 'erotic'.

Often depicted in Greek art bearing wings and holding his silver bow and arrow, Eros is thought to ignite sexual desire. His perceived personality has changed in art and literature as time has marched on: he appears as a strapping young man in earlier Greek portrayals and since then his character became more mischievous and playful, until Roman (and later) art has depicted him as a rotund baby Cupid who flew around firing arrows at Gods and mortals to fall in love with each other. The iconography of Eros and the arrow through the heart is still widely used today.

Athena

Athena is one of the most revered and likeable goddesses in Greek mythology. Unlike many of her contemporaries, she tended not to act vengefully or to take her anger out on mere mortals. She came to resemble the embodiment of all things noble in Greek culture, from wisdom and honesty, to bravery and ferocity in war. She first emerged from Zeus' head (after he had swallowed her pregnant mother Metis) fully clad in armour and ready for action.

This collection of wonderful traits made Athena the goddess of law and justice, wisdom and courage, and, as such, she acted as a general guardian angel to key characters in both Greek and Roman literature (helping Odysseus and Aeneas out of difficult situations by making them stronger, taller, invisible or disguised, as the scenario required).

The city at the heart of the Greek civilization still bears her name, and her purity as the virgin goddess is celebrated in the Parthenon ('parthenos' means 'virgin' in Greek) that dominates the city's skyline. Both she and Poseidon vied to have the great city dedicated to them. His campaign began first when he struck down his trident to allow seawater to pour from a source in the city; Athena outdid him by planting the first olive tree. Twelve gods presided over the decision and awarded Athena the honour, much to Poseidon's dismay. Depending on which version of the myth you read, Poseidon either did or didn't flood the city with seawater in revenge.

Because of various myths associated with Athena, she is depicted variously in Greek art by her shield, symbols of the olive tree or the wise owl.

Ares

Son of Zeus and Hera, Ares is the personification of war and the brute lust for battle and, while not the only Greek god associated with war, he occupies a specific role within it. While Hephaestus, for example, concerned himself with the art of creating armour and weaponry, Athena offered guidance to the Greeks and provided them with a justification for war.

Recounts of war in Greek literature feature heavily the influence of Ares' wrath. In one story, Cadmus, the founder of the Greek city Thebes, and his band of men went in search of Cadmus' sister Europa, who had been abducted by Zeus. Advised to follow the first cow they came across, Cadmus and his tribe set off on their trip. They soon encountered a spring that was guarded by a snake (who, rather worryingly, happened to be an offspring of Ares), which then killed Cadmus' band of men. In retaliation, Cadmus killed the snake with a rock.

Athena advised Cadmus to remove some of the snake's teeth and bury them in the soil, and from this an army of men – known as the Spartoi – emerged and helped Cadmus to found the city of Thebes. Unfortunately for Cadmus, Ares wrecked his revenge for the slaying of the snake by forcing him to work as his slave for an entire year. Although Cadmus went on to take Ares' daughter, Harmonia, as his wife, the two of them were turned later into snakes themselves.

Hades

Ruler of the underworld, Hades is, not unsurprisingly, perceived as an angry sort. His name is also used to refer to the underworld itself, and it is here that everyone is consigned to after death. Rather than the heaven and hell of Christianity, the Greeks had just one place for the dead, although there are many different places within Hades, some of which are far more desirable than others.

According to Greek mythology, very few managed to enter Hades and return to earth alive, which is not surprising given the difficult journey it entailed. It began with an excursion by ferry across the black river Acheron, with the deity Charon acting as oarsman. His services didn't come cheap, and it is for this reason that the Greeks – and the Romans – placed a coin in the mouth of the dear departed before they were cremated.

On the other side of the Acheron, the situation

deteriorated further. The huge and violent three-headed dog Cerberus (a figure that has cropped up in literature ever since, and even had a cameo in the first *Harry Potter* book) guarded the passage to the region of Erebus, where lay the river Lethe – from which the dead souls drank in order to forget their earthly lives. In front of the palace of Hades, all entrants' lives were judged, and the outcome of this decision determined where they would spend eternity. Tartarus was the home for horrendous punishment and the fields of Elysium (which gave their name to one of the most prominent roads in Paris, the Champs-Élysées) the opportunity to reside joyfully among the grass and flowers.

Hephaestus

Hephaestus is the god of fire, volcanoes, metalwork and sculpture and he can be recognized in Greek art by the hammer and tongs he carries and by his penchant for riding a donkey. It was the highest honour to receive a set of armour made by him personally, as Achilles did before he went into battle in Homer's *Iliad*. Hephaestus also created the armoury for the remaining gods on Mount Olympus.

In contrast to the skill and intricate nature of his handiwork, Hephaestus is known as a lame god. Reports vary, but we do know that he had a slightly deformed leg following a fall from the top of Mount Olympus right down to ground level.

Other stories suggest his leg was withered from birth, and his mother Hera, disgusted at her son's deformity, flung him down to earth. There, Hephaestus landed in the sea and was retrieved, rather fortunately, and raised by Eurynome and Thetis (mother of Achilles) on the volcanic island of Lemnos – where he honed his skill as a master craftsman.

Another version of the myth sees Hephaestus acquiring his leg injury after being flung from the peak of Mount Olympus as a fully-grown god, which resulted in his leg injury. According to this legend, Zeus was angry at his wife Hera for setting a storm on Heracles as he returned from Troy, and so, as punishment, Zeus hung Hera in chains from Olympus. When Hephaestus went to his mother's rescue, Zeus grabbed him by the leg and flung him down the mountain. His fall lasted for an entire day, ending on the island of Lemnos, just as the sun was setting.

Cronos

Although Zeus is the father of the gods, he was the son of
Cronos, who himself was the offspring of Gaia (the earth)
and Uranus (the sky). Cronos married his sister Rhea and
together they produced the gods and goddesses of Mount
Olympus, including, in addition to Zeus, Hera (who also
became Zeus' wife), Hades and Poseidon, among others.

Cronos took over power of the heavens from his father
Uranus by castrating him with a jagged-toothed sickle.
After a prophecy revealed he too would face the same fate
at the hands of his own sons, Cronos took matters into his
own hands by swallowing each child that Rhea produced.
Only the youngest son, Zeus, avoided this same fate when
Rhea managed to give birth to him in secret in a mountain
cave in Crete. To deceive her husband, Rhea gave him a
rock covered up in a blanket under the pretence it was
their son, which Cronos quickly devoured in one gulp.

Once Zeus came of age, he liberated his grown siblings
from Cronos' belly. And, following a vicious ten-year war
against his father's generation of Greek gods, the Titans,
Zeus was victorious, and Cronos and his fellow Titans
were driven down into Tartarus in the underworld.
The way was paved for the next generation of gods:
the Olympians.

Gaia

As the goddess of earth and the mother of all, Gaia is the Greek gods' matriarchal figure. It was from her unions with Uranus (the sky), Pontus (the sea) and Tartarus (the underworld) that all other gods were created. There are elements of the 'earth mother' figure in many other belief systems, and it is thought her existence in Greek culture is a mythological hangover from an earlier time.

Despite her motherly role, Gaia was not averse to trouble. It was she who helped her son Cronos overthrow and castrate Uranus. And when she had tired of Cronos' antics she assisted her grandson, Zeus, in his overthrow of the Titans to become leader of the gods. Her work did not stop there. Angry that Zeus had committed Cronos to the underworld, Gaia enlisted the help of the Gigantes and the monster Typhoeus to despatch with Zeus, too. However, her grandson was too great a match.

The Muses

In Greek mythology, the Titan goddess Mnemosyne was the personification of memory (her name deriving from the Greek word for 'mindful', and which is perpetuated in English words such as 'mnemonic'). She was also the mother of the Muses, the nine sisters who inspired all the arts, following a nine-day romance with Zeus.

MUSE	AREA OF INSPIRATION	OFTEN SEEN CARRYING
Calliope	Muse of Epic Poetry	a writing tablet
Clio	Muse of History	scrolls
Erato	Muse of Lyric Poetry	a cithara (an instrument of the lyre family)
Euterpe	Muse of Music	a flute-like instrument
Melpomene	Muse of Tragedy	a tragic mask
Polyhymnia	Muse of Hymns	a veil
Terpsichore	Muse of Light Verse and Dance	a lyre
Thalia	Muse of Comedy	a comic mask
Urania	Muse of Astronomy	a globe or compass

Many of the great pieces of Greek – and Roman – literature open with an invocation to the Muses to inspire the poet in his or her telling of a particular myth. The concept of writers and artists – and others, such as astronomers – being inspired by Muses continued in Western art and literature for many centuries, as in the Prologue to Act I of Shakespeare's *King Henry V*, which begins, 'O! for a Muse of fire, that would ascend / The brightest heaven of invention.'

Even today, fashion designers speak of having a 'muse' in one particular model or celebrity, whose body shape, personality or style they will use as inspiration in their development of new designs.

Adonis

Yet another Greek god associated with the enduring theme of love and desire, Adonis, the god of plants and rebirth, was a beautiful man who, even as a youngster, was able to attract the attentions of the goddess of love, Aphrodite. With the young Adonis under her charge, Aphrodite gave him to Persephone, goddess of spring and queen of the underworld (see below), to look after in her absence.

Persephone, too, became enamoured with Adonis and was reluctant to return him to Aphrodite when the time came. A dispute ensued, settled only by Zeus' decree that Adonis split his time equally between Aphrodite, Persephone and a destination of his choosing. Unfortunately for Persephone, Adonis made his allegiances clear when he chose to spend his free time with Aphrodite – a union that so angered Aphrodite's husband Ares that he disguised himself as a wild boar and killed Adonis in a jealous rage. He died in Aphrodite's arms.

Persephone

A rather sad character, Persephone is the goddess of spring and the daughter of Zeus and Demeter, and her story is used to explain the changing of the seasons. Although Persephone's mother tried hard to shield her daughter from the many amorous godly suitors, her efforts were thwarted when one afternoon while Persephone was happily picking flowers in a field, Hades, god of the underworld, appeared and abducted Persephone and took her as his wife.

Angry at this violation, Demeter demanded Hades return her daughter. Hades eventually relented, but, by this stage, Persephone had tasted her husband's delicious pomegranate fruits, and, as such, was bound to return there as his wife and queen of the underworld for half the year. In her absence, the mortal world was plunged into winter and spring only reappeared when she returned bi-annually to ground level.

Dione

Zeus is thought to have sired children with up to approximately sixty different goddesses and women, one of whom was Dione. Her name, quite simply, is a female version of 'Zeus' – derived from the same root from which we get the words 'divine', 'deity', 'Diana' and 'Jupiter'. She is the mother of Aphrodite – who herself is one of the very ancient goddesses – and, as such, Dione's appearance in Greek mythology is similar to that of earth mother Gaia.

Dione's appearances in ancient texts are fleeting, but in the few words attributed to her she exposes a rarely seen aspect of the Greek gods' vulnerability. After her daughter, Aphrodite, was wounded in the War of Troy while trying to protect her own son, Aeneas (more on him on page 176), she returned to her mother on Mount Olympus for comfort. As Dione took care of Aphrodite, she reminded her that immortals too have their weaknesses. To illustrate her point, she told Aphrodite of an incident when the war god Ares was once held prisoner inside a cauldron by two brutish brother giants, and it was only after the intervention of the giants' stepmother, who enlisted the help of Hermes, that the war god was rescued. Dione also tells how the great gods Hera and Hades were once injured by Heracles' weapons.

HEROES, HEROINES, VILLAINS AND MONSTERS

You will find you are familiar with many of these heroes of Greek mythology.

Heracles (Hercules)

Heracles is known more widely by his Roman name Hercules, and was respected for his size and strength, his quick wit and his skill as a fighter. He made the transition from mythical warrior hero to the status of immortal god, and was worshipped as such later on. He was the son of Zeus and the mortal Alcmene (after Zeus disguised himself as her husband), and it is said that Zeus' wife, Hera, focused her energies on hating and being jealous of Heracles for this reason.

Driven mad by Hera, Heracles murderd his children.

To atone for his grave behaviour, he was required to carry out twelve near-impossible heroic tasks devised by his nemesis, Eurystheus, who had deposed him as king. The completion of these tasks would cleanse Heracles' soul and propel him into immortality.

These myths originate from the Greeks' interest in astrology: it is thought that each of the twelve labours once referred to an animal seen in the night-time constellations – some of which we still use today. For more on our modern-day constellations and the myths associated with them see pages 174–84.

THE TWELVE LABOURS OF HERACLES

1. Kill the Nemean Lion

A huge creature was wreaking havoc in Nemea: a lion whose hide was thought to be impenetrable. Heracles' first task was to kill it. Heracles was able to corner the beast and wrestle it to the ground, whereupon he took its pelt (and he is often depicted in Greek art and sculpture wearing the hide). Hera immortalized the lion in the constellation Leo.

2. Slay the Lernaean Hydra

The Hydra was a nine-headed sea snake, which Heracles was sent to destroy. But each time he cut off one of its heads, two more would grow in its place, making the task insurmountable. To make matters worse, the Hydra was assisted by a giant crab, which further impeded Heracles' efforts. Not to be outsmarted, with the help of his nephew, Iolaus, Heracles set a burning torch onto the severed necks of the Hydra, preventing further heads from growing. He also killed the crab by squashing it underfoot. Both beasts were then placed into the stars by Hera as the Hydra and Cancer constellations.

3. Capture the Cerynitian Hind

The next task was to retrieve the Cerynitian Hind, a golden-horned deer sacred to the goddess Artemis. After chasing the animal for an entire year, Heracles finally managed to get hold of it, but only after a significant struggle during which one of the animal's sacred horns came unstuck. Despite her annoyance at this minor destruction, Artemis allowed Heracles to borrow the animal for his remaining his quests.

4. Capture the Erymanthean Boar

Heracles pursued this huge beast around the snowy sides of Mount Erymanthos, until he was able to capture it in a net and bring it back to Eurystheus – who was so startled by the creature that he jumped into a huge jar to hide.

5. Clean the Augean Stables

King Augeas of Elis kept a huge herd of 1,000 cattle, and Heracles' task was to clean out the stables – a task that had not been undertaken in several decades. Heracles set about his task by diverting nearby rivers to flow through the stables. After Augeas failed to honour his promise to give 100 of the cattle to Heracles if he completed the task in one day, Heracles launched an attack on Elis. When he was eventually victorious, it is said that he started the first Olympic Games in celebration.

6. Kill the Stymphalian Birds

These man-eating beasts terrorized Lake Stymphalis in Arcadia. Heracles was able to kill them one by one with his bow and arrow, having first startled them into the air by using a rattle. It is thought they are represented by the constellations Aquila (eagle) and Cygnus (swan), which lie in the night sky either side of Sagitta (representing Heracles' arrow).

7. Capture the Cretan Bull

This huge white bull was sent to Crete from the sea by Poseidon, where it seduced King Minos' wife, Pasiphaë. She even had a fake wooden cow created in which she could submerge herself to fulfil her desires, after which she mothered the half-man half-beast Minotaur (see page 163, and the story of Europa [page 165] for a similar tale). Heracles was, of course, successful in his attempt to capture the bull, which is remembered as the Taurus constellation.

8. Steal the Mares of Diomedes

Next in Heracles' list of tasks was to steal the horses of the violent King Diomedes. Heracles took with him a few young companions to help, including his favoured companion Abderus, whose job it was to look after the horses while Heracles and the others attended to Diomedes. Unfortunately, Heracles and his men were unaware that the horses were ferocious, flesh-eating maniacs, and so when they returned they found Abderus had been killed. Heracles held the lifeless body in his arms and wept. He then created a tomb for the boy, upon which site the city of Abdera was founded many years later. After binding the horses' mouths shut, Heracles and his remaining companions were able to return them to King Eurystheus.

9. Get the Girdle of Hippolyta

Hippolyta was queen of the Amazons – a group of brutal female warriors – and she was the proud owner of a belt made by Ares, the god of war. Although Hippolyta was quite willing to hand over the belt to Heracles, which Eurystheus' daughter had her keen eye on, Hera started a rumour among the Amazons that Heracles was there to steal the queen herself. Chaos ensued. After the Amazons attacked Heracles, he retaliated by killing Hippolyta and stealing the belt.

10. Steal the Cattle of Geryon

A three-headed, three-bodied monster, Geryon resided on the island of Erytheia, where he kept a herd of cows that had been coloured red by the setting sun of the west. Heracles travelled to the island in a golden cup-boat given to him by Helios, the sun god, whereupon he set about his task. Heracles first killed the cattle-herder Euyrition, followed by the two-headed guard dog Orthrus, and used a bow dipped in the blood of the Hydra (see page 153) to kill Geryon. He faced a bit of a task in returning the cattle to Eurystheus – not helped by Hera placing a gadfly in the herd to disrupt and disperse them – but he succeeded in the end.

But Heracles then faced further struggle: although Eurystheus had initially told him that he had just ten tasks to complete, he decided to add two more – on the basis that Heracles had received help with killing the Hydra, and had received payment in cows in the Augean stables. Undeterred, Heracles pressed on.

11. Steal the Apples of Hesperides

The Hesperides were three goddesses who looked after a tree of golden apples and their story relates to the setting sun. ('Hesperos' in Greek means 'evening', and the word is associated with anything to do with the golden sunset and the west.) The story of Heracles' triumph varies according to which version you read. One story suggests Heracles slew the hundred-headed serpent that guarded the tree and before making off with a punnet of apples. Another myth tells how he offered to hold up the whole world for Atlas in exchange for his collecting the apples (in this version,

Atlas is related to the Hesperides, which means he already has them onside). When Atlas returned with the apples, he seemed happy for Heracles to continue holding up the world. Surprisingly, Heracles agreed, but on one condition: Atlas relieve him temporarily so he could adjust his cloak to make it more comfortable . . . at which point Heracles made an inevitable dash, golden apples in hand.

12. Fetch Cerberus

Of all the labours of Heracles, this was undoubtedly the toughest. Cerberus was the vicious three-headed guard dog in the underworld (see more on Hades on page 141), and certainly not the sort of beast you'd happily take out on a leash. Cerberus was the sibling of the Hydra as well as of Orthrus, the two-headed guard dog of Geryon's cattle. He was also the uncle to the Nemean Lion.

As the first mortal to attempt a round-trip to Hades, Heracles first visited a priest who conducted rituals by invoking the myth of Persephone (see page 149). Heracles climbed down into the underworld, eventually overpowering Cerberus with his bare hands and bringing him up to Eurystheus. Unlike many of Heracles' other conquests, Cerberus was later returned to Hades unharmed.

Perseus and Medusa

King Acrisius of Argos was once told by an oracle that he would be killed by the son of his daughter Danae, which led the king to lock her away from the prying eyes of the world's suitors. Despite this intervention, Zeus came in disguise as a golden shower and impregnated Danae. When she gave birth to her son, Perseus, the two were cast off to sea by Acrisius, landing on the island of Seriphus.

As a grown man, Perseus was commanded by King Polydectes to bring back the head of Medusa – the fearsome beast with serpents lashing out of her head. One look at her would turn you to stone (the literal meaning of the word 'petrify'), but such warnings did not stop Perseus. With the help of the goddess Athena, Perseus hatched a plan of attack, equipped with Athena's mirrored shield. His journey saw him visiting the Graiai – three old, haggard, witch-like sisters who shared one eye and one tooth, and who have appeared across literature and film, such as in Shakespeare's *Macbeth* and any number of witch-related movies (*Hocus Pocus*, *The Witches of Eastwick* and *Stardust* to name just three).

Eventually, Perseus reached Medusa and, using the mirrored shield to direct his weapons, was able to kill her and remove her head without looking at her and risking petrifaction. He returned to Seriphus and revealed the head to King Polydectes, which immediately turned the king to stone.

Perseus returned to his homeland and successfully overthrew his grandfather, who flees. Much later, the oracle's prophecy is finally realized when at a ceremonial games Perseus' errant discus kills the his grandfather.

Midas

The origin of this well-known tale was used by the Greeks to explain the presence of gold in the Pactolus river on what is now the Turkish coast of the Aegean Sea. Following a favour, King Midas was granted one wish by the god Dionysus. Without a moment's pause, the king wished that everything he touched turned to gold.

For a while, life was wonderful: Midas freely indulged his new found powers, turning his chariots, livestock and his garden into useless – but valuable – lumps of gleaming gold. But this joy was short-lived, however, as King Midas soon realized the difficulties of having every item of food and drink turned to glistening metal. Events took a turn for the worse when, having taken his daughter by the hand to demonstrate his new party trick, his horror was complete: she turned to gold. Thankfully, Dionysus listened to Midas' disgusted regret and allowed him to wash away his new skill in the Pactolus river, after which all of his possessions, including his daughter, were returned to their original state.

'The Midas touch' is a phrase often attributed now to successful businesspeople in a complimentary manner. Rather alarmingly, we use it only to refer to positive short-term gain and we seem to have forgotten that Midas nearly starved to death, temporarily killed his daughter and immediately regretted his power.

Croesus

A wonderful offshoot of Midas' dalliance with alchemy is that the gold in the Pactolus river went on to make another man very rich indeed. The stories of Croesus blur happily between fact and myth; we know that he was indeed the last King of Lydia, ruling over much of modern-day Turkey in the sixth century BC. But because of his colossal wealth he soon became a character of legend, which became more fantastical as time went on – and within a few centuries the myths around him were no longer necessarily placed in the right chronology.

One story involving the king tells how he was visited by travelling Athenian Solon. Croesus showed off all of his wonderful possessions and riches, and asked whether Solon knew of anyone who could be more blessed than he. Not being a man of tact, Solon answered that he knew of three others who were more blessed than Croesus – mere commoners who had passed their lives in brave and noble ways, and who had all died having lived a good life, despite having no riches. Solon told the king it was only after someone had died that you could look back to see whether or not they should be thought of as the most blessed person.

And the real King Croesus did indeed become a touch too sure of himself when he decided in 547 BC to launch a pre-emptive strike against the Persians, who seemed to be on a path of growth. In seeking advice from several oracles before the attack, Croesus was told that if he were to fight the Persians it would result in the destruction of a great empire. Sadly for Croesus, it was his own empire that he would destroy.

Theseus and the Minotaur

Another mythical hero that came to embody all things Greek, manly and brave, Theseus is the son of King Aegeus of Athens and the sea god Poseidon, having both copulated with Aethra. His dual paternity bestowed upon him a prince-like stature as well as lending him a touch of the divine, which enabled him to call upon the gods for help when needed.

Greece as we know it today didn't exist as one entity, and instead was a collection of many different city-states, each with its own king, but nonetheless unified through similar languages centred on Athens. In Crete, King Minos was a fearful ruler, and, following an altercation with Athens, he demanded that seven young men and seven young women should each year board a black-sailed ship to Crete to be sacrificed to the Minotaur. Half-man and half-bull, the beast was the result of a union between a bull and either Europa or Pasiphaë (according to which myth you read), and it lived hidden away in King Minos' inescapable labyrinth.

Theseus endeavoured to put an end to this tradition and become a hero among his people, and so he volunteered himself as one of the seven young men. When in Minos' palace in Knossos, Theseus was visited by the king's daughter Ariadne. She gave to him a ball of silk thread and told him to unwind it as he travelled through the labyrinth to help him find his way out. Theseus did as she suggested and bravely killed the Minotaur. Upon leaving the palace triumphantly, Theseus decided to take Ariadne home with him, but his attempts were thwarted by the god Dionysus, who instructed him to leave her on the island of Naxos since the god wanted her for his own bride.

In his grief, Theseus returned to Athens and forgot to change the sails of the ship from black to white. King Aegeus saw the ship approaching from a distance and feared the worst. Without waiting to confirm his concerns, he hurled himself into the sea that now bears his name.

Theseus then became king of Athens, and unified the Attic states into one notional country. Since this unification actually took place over a number of centuries, we can assume the myth of Theseus to be an allegory of the 'Greekness' he embodied. Minos was known for his barbaric and draconian punishments, so it is easy to see how a foreign king in a huge sprawling palace could be muddled into a mythical beast living in a confusing labyrinth (of which there is no evidence in Knossos). In slaying the barbaric non-Greek monster and overcoming the Cretan king, the hero Theseus acts as a perfectly virile personification of the Greek people.

Europa

Europa's name has been bestowed not only on one of the moons of Jupiter (the planet) but also on the continent of Europe. She was by all accounts a very pretty young girl of the nobility – so pretty, in fact, that Zeus felt the urge to disguise himself as a docile white bull in order to seduce her.

Europa approached the seemingly unthreatening animal and began to caress it and decorate it with flowers. Eventually, she decided to climb upon its back, at which point Zeus ran at full speed into the sea and swam all the way to Crete, with the girl still mounted on top.

A procession of nymphs, spirits and other gods joined them on their journey and encouraged Europa to consider that this was no ordinary white bull; she quickly cottoned on to the idea that he might be a god.

By Zeus, she bore a three sons, including King Minos of Crete, who was famous for his brutality and possession of the mythical Minotaur (see above). Europa was also the sister of Cadmus, who, during his search for his abducted sister, had incurred the wrath of Ares, as seen earlier in this chapter (on page 140).

Icarus

The story of Icarus and his father craftsman Daedalus is a moral one, acting as a heartbreaking way to warn us of the importance of humility. There are similarities between this myth and the Chinese Kua Fu (see page 72), showing the way in which different civilizations have devised similar allegorical tales to demonstrate universal life lessons.

According to Greek mythology, Icarus and Daedalus were held captive inside King Minos' great labyrinth in Crete, which Daedalus had built for the king. Daedalus had been the one to give Minos' daughter, Ariadne, the ball of string that helped Theseus find his way out of the labyrinth (see page 164). Despite not knowing the way out of his own construction, Daedalus is said to have had great ingenuity, and skilfully cobbled together two sets of wings from feathers held together with wax for him and his son to make their escape away from Crete.

Daedalus warned his son not to fly too close to the sun, to follow him closely and avoid making his own path. Needless to say, Icarus failed to heed his father's advice and flew higher and higher in the sky. But the closer he got to the sun, the warmer the wax became, until he could flap no more and fell soaring into the sea. There exists today an island called Ikaria, which is sited in an area of the Aegean Sea known as the Ikarian Sea – the place at which Icarus is said to have entered so many years ago.

Chapter 8:

Roman Mythology

WHO WERE THE ROMANS?

More than any other civilization, the Romans can lay claim to having had the biggest impact on modern Western society. And yet, much of what they introduced had, in fact, been acquired from the Greeks – from the gods of Greek mythology, to its law, art, philosophy, literature, society, theatre and technology.

Roman civilization lasted for more than a thousand years, encompassing at its height much of western and northern Europe, North Africa and the Middle East. What began as a group of settlements joined together to form the city of Rome by 600 BC. In 509 BC, it became a republic, ruled by two consuls elected from the senate, and, growing in strength, Rome soon overpowered the other settlers on the Italian peninsular.

By 146 BC, Rome had acquired her first overseas territories – Sicily, Spain and North Africa – and the Macedonian wars that followed saw further acquisitions in Macedonia, Greece and Asia Minor. In 27 BC, Julius Caesar's son became the first emperor of Rome and imperial rule was to continue for the next 400 years.

By the second century AD, the Roman Empire covered all of the Mediterranean, most of western and southern Europe and even extended across what is modern-day Turkey, Israel, Egypt, Iraq, Iran and parts of Saudi Arabia. However, in its dying days, the empire's sheer size made it vulnerable to attack from northern Europe. By AD 455, Germanic tribes had sacked Rome itself and, in AD 476, the last Roman Emperor, Romulus Augustus, abdicated, signalling the collapse of the empire.

Gods and Goddesses

The Romans were so enamoured with Greek mythology they adopted its pantheon of gods and goddesses and their accompanying stories. In fact, much of what we know about Greek mythology actually comes from Latin literature. As such, rather than recount the myths already told in Chapter 7 below is a conversion table of the Greek and Latin names. You will notice that the planets in our solar system have all been named after the top Roman gods (with the exception of Earth).

GREEK NAME	LATIN EQUIVALENT	WHO'S WHO
Aphrodite	Venus	Goddess of love and beauty
Apollo	Apollo	God of music, the sun, archery
Ares	Mars	God of war
Artemis	Diana	Goddess of hunting, fertility
Athena	Minerva	Goddess of wisdom, courage, protection
Cronos	Saturn	God of the sky, ruler of the Titans
Demeter	Ceres	Goddess of agriculture (cf. English 'cereal')
Dionysus	Bacchus	God of wine
Eros	Cupid	God of love and desire
Hades	Pluto	God of the underworld
Hephaestus	Vulcan	God of fire, volcanoes, weaponry
Hera	Juno	Wife of Zeus / Jupiter
Heracles	Hercules	General manly hero and demigod
Hermes	Mercury	Messenger of the gods, with winged sandals
Persephone	Proserpina	Wife of Hades / Pluto
Poseidon	Neptune	God of the sea
Uranus	Uranus	The sky, father of the Titans
Zeus	Jupiter	Ruler of the gods, adept with a lightning bolt

THE ORIGINS OF ROME: PICK A STORY

Stories differ regarding the beginnings of the great city of Rome, which was the beating heart of the Roman's colossal empire that ruled the Mediterranean for 2,000 years. The earlier myths tend to use the story of the twins Romulus and Remus who were brought up by a wolf to demonstrate the founding of the city of Rome, but later myths, such as Virgil's poem about Aeneas, depict a Trojan hero descended directly from the gods as the city's noble founder. (Virgil manages to insert Romulus and Remus as a footnote into his story, so as not to disquiet the traditionalists.)

Romulus and Remus

Most of us might be able to recall the story of the twins brought up by a wolf, but perhaps not how (or why) the myth was chosen to depict the origins of Rome. After the twin brothers were deserted by their father, Mars, the god of violent war, they were brought up in the woods by a wolf (an icon of fear).

But their new-found stability was not to last long because in 753 BC, Romulus killed his brother in an argument and founded a city to celebrate, to which he gave his own name. In an effort to populate his newly established city, Romulus began to steal women against their will from nearby region of Sabinum – a scene captured in countless pieces of Renaissance art as The Rape of the Sabine Women.

It seems strange that such a proud civilization came from such inauspicious beginnings, but perhaps it is this sense of arrogant pride that made the Romans so successful: their feeling of superiority allowed them to expand the empire with great strength. And, with such a bold myth as their starting point, the Romans perhaps gave the population a sense of entitlement that worked in the empire's favour.

Aeneas

In 29 BC, Augustus Caesar, the first official emperor of the Roman Empire, commissioned Virgil to write an epic poem of the founding of Rome. The empire had been the victim of years of external strife and civil war, following a series of dictatorships that gave way to the collapse of the Roman Republic and its rebirth as the empire. Augustus Caesar wanted a piece of literature to instil a sense of pride in Rome and cement his precarious position by telling the story of city's beginnings. The poem also conveniently links Augustus and his family by heritage to the very founders of the city, never mind that he was actually adopted by Julius Caesar.

In *The Aeneid*, Virgil tells of the Trojan hero Aeneas as he travelled away from defeat by the Greeks at the ten-year War of Troy to find a new home in Italy. The legend borrows unapologetically from the two great works of Greek poet Homer, *The Iliad* and *The Odyssey* (deemed to be the first compositions ever committed to writing in the Western world). Virgil uses the Greek myths that Roman citizens would have grown up with and makes them uniquely and boldly Roman – aligning the new Roman Empire with the very ancient stories told over many generations around the Mediterranean.

The most moving tale within *The Aeneid* is that of Aeneas and Dido. She is the Queen of Carthage who falls in love with Aeneas on his journey to Italy. Venus (goddess of love, and also Aeneas' mother) encourages this burgeoning romance by conjuring up a storm, which sees the two seek shelter together in a cave.

But ultimately, Aeneas is reminded by Jupiter's messenger Mercury that his duty is to found Rome, and that he must leave behind his love and carnal urges for Dido if he is to fulfil his fate. Aeneas explains to Dido that he must go, and his ships set sail. In her pain, the queen wisely prophesies an everlasting conflict between Carthage and the future Rome, and then kills herself using a sword Aeneas had given her.

Her light from her burning pyre is seen by Aeneas as his fleet sails away, and he knows then what she has done. *The Aeneid* emotive passages about Dido's heartache and subsequent suicide make this one of the great love stories of Western literature. Aeneas later meets his former flame in the underworld and tries to explain his actions, but her ghost remains chillingly silent, refusing to look him in the eyes.

THE SIGNS OF THE ZODIAC

The signs of the zodiac are a wonderful example of how myths can spread from one civilization to another. The term 'zodiac' originally comes from a Greek phrase meaning a 'circle of animals', which refers to the circular astrological chart that is split into twelve sections, each with its own animalistic representation. But this concept predates the Greeks even, seen nearly 3,000 years ago with the Sumerians and Babylonian (in modern-day Iraq). Even some of the same animal characters were used in those earliest versions.

Every civilization has looked to the stars in wonder, and humans have created many wonderful stories for the shapes we see in them and in their movement across our skyline. It is through this stargazing that we have developed as navigators both on our own planet and beyond it.

The Greeks had their own interpretations of the constellations, some of which are included here, and some of which have their own origin myths from the Labours of Heracles (see page 152). The Romans adopted and subsequently Romanized the names, and, several thousand years, later they are still showing their influence in newspaper horoscopes the world over. The Babylonians would be pleased.

Latin name (used in English)	English translation	Why?
Aries	Ram	There have been many goat-related myths across the world, but the Greeks and Romans settled on the golden-fleeced ram, the coat of which Jason and his Argonauts was tasked to steal from King Aeetes of Colchis.
Taurus	Bull	This constellation is believed to have been identified as looking like a bull from as staggeringly far back as 15,000 BC. The Greek and Roman myth of the constellation was about either Jupiter disguised as a bull to seduce Europa, or about Heracles' capture of the Cretan Bull (see page 155).

Latin name (used in English)	English translation	Why?
Gemini	Twins	The twins Castor and Pollux can be seen as stick men drawn into the stars. They are brothers of Helen of Troy (whose abduction started the great War of Troy) and Clytemnestra (who murdered her husband Agamemnon after the war). The two boys are associated with horsemanship and navigation. Pollux and Helen emerged from one egg when Zeus disguised himself as a swan to rape their mother Leda, and from another egg emerged Castor and Clytemnestra, fathered by Tyndareus. Therefore, only Pollux was immortal, but Zeus granted his brother immortality in the stars.
Cancer	Crab	The crab has a rather uninspiring role to play in classical mythology, appearing as a snapping accomplice to the Lernaean Hydra that Hercules must defeat (see page 153). Hercules dispatches the beast by squishing it underfoot – and now it resides in the stars.
Leo	Lion	The lion is another shape recognized very early on – by the Mesopotamians as early as 4000 BC. The Greeks and Romans associate it with the myth of Hercules overcoming the Nemean Lion (see page 152).

Latin name (used in English)	English translation	Why?
Virgo	Virgin	This constellation shows a female figure in the night sky. As such, she has been associated with a variety of characters. Earlier Babylonians associated these stars with agricultural fertility, and that remains with the Romans, who associate the female form with Ceres (goddess of agriculture) and depicted her carrying a frond. Other myths name the constellation as Justitia (goddess of justice), with her close proximity to the scales of justice in neighbouring constellation Libra.
Libra	Scales	The stars that make up the scales in the sky used to be the claws of the Greek Scorpio constellation, but the Romans turned the claws into its own distinct constellation of balancing scales. (A little creative licence is needed when observing shapes in the stars.) The aspect of Earth against the stars changes over time, so Libra used to be visible in the sky during the autumn equinox – with the equal balance of night and day fitting well with this imagery. In the modern day, we are in Virgo when we reach this equinox.

Latin name (used in English)	English translation	Why?
Scorpio	Scorpion	The scorpion, whether dismembered by the Romans or not, lies close to the constellation of Orion and it rises in the night sky just as the stars of Orion set on the horizon. As such, the scorpion is seen as an adversary from which he is running away – either sent by Diana in retaliation for Orion's unwanted advances, or sent by the Earth in response to his boast that he could slay any beast.
Sagittarius	Archer	This constellation depicts a centaur – the torso of a man and the body and legs of a horse – aiming his bow and arrow at the neighbouring scorpion.
Capricorn	Horned goat/fish	This half-goat half-fish figure appears on the winter solstice on 21 December. As such, he has resembled the start of winter for many millennia before the Greeks or Romans adopted the association. They called him Pan (Greek) or Faunus (Roman), and the myth goes that he was hiding from the monster Typhon, who was sent to fight the gods. He dipped into the Nile and changed his bottom half to that of a fish to help his escape. Jupiter immortalized him in the stars as gratitude for various good deeds he had done for the gods.

Latin name (used in English)	English translation	Why?
Aquarius	Water-bearer	With one of the most ambitious interpretations, this constellation depicts a young man pouring water from an amphora jug. In classical mythology, he is associated with a young boy called Ganymede (Greek) or Catamitus (the Latin transliteration). Zeus was enamoured with as young boy and so disguised himself as an eagle to abduct the boy and take him to Mount Olympus, where he became the gods' cup-bearer. This story is depicted by the nearby constellation of Aquila (Latin for 'eagle').
Pisces	Fish	The two fish depicted here joined by a cord are said to represent Venus and her son Cupid as they escaped the terrible monster Typhon, who was sent to kill the gods. While Faunus (the Capricorn) went for a dip in the Nile to escape, this pair transformed themselves entirely into fish.

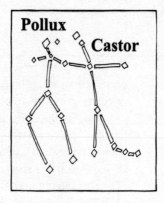

The Gemini Constellation

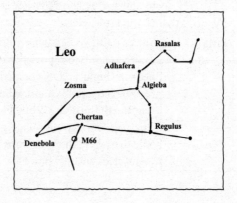

The Leo Constellation

HEROES AND HEROINES

These Roman tales owe much to Greek mythology.

Orpheus and Eurydice

This tragic love story is told most beautifully by Ovid in his poetry compilation *Metamorphoses*, in which he provides a host of myths to explain everything from the origins of the butterfly to the laurel tree.

Orpheus and Eurydice were very much in love, but soon after they were married she was bitten by a snake and died. Orpheus was overwhelmed with grief and felt he had nothing to live for other than the mesmerizing song of his lyre. Orpheus made the bold journey into Hades (or Aides, as the Romans called it) and implored Pluto and Proserpina with his entrancing music to return his wife to the realm of the living. His music was so staggeringly beautiful that the whole of the underworld stopped for a moment.

They were so moved that Proserpina could not refuse – on one condition: that Orpheus lead his wife all the way up to the mortal world without looking at her once, and only set eye on her once they had arrived. Together, the reunited pair made the long climb up the steep and dark path, with Eurydice limping behind.

As they neared the entrance to Hades, the darkness gradually faded and Orpheus was so desperate to make sure his wife made it over the threshold that he looked back. He knew immediately it was too soon, and straight away Eurydice sank back into the underworld muttering a faint 'farewell' to her former flame. Orpheus reached out to touch her three times, but three times his hands went through nothingness where she had once stood.

Orpheus had lost his wife twice and was not allowed to re-enter the underworld. With nothing left to live for, he traipsed about with his lyre waiting for his fate, which arrived in the form of a group of female spirits called the Maenades. They set about tearing poor Orpheus limb from limb, after which they created a shrine for him at the base of Mount Olympus. Even now, the song of the nightingales at this site is said to be the most beautiful in the world.

The Trojan Horse

Another distinctly Greek tale that is retold in more detail in Virgil's *Aeneid* (more on that previously on page 176).

The story of the Trojan Horse takes place towards the end of the ten-year War of Troy, in which the Greeks tried to retrieve Helen, daughter of Zeus and the wife of King Menelaus of Sparta in Greece, who had been gifted to Paris of Troy by the goddess Venus. The war had been raging for almost a decade but the walled city of Troy looked to remain fighting fit.

A cunning plan was hatched by the Greeks: they retreated in their hundreds of ships until they were just out of sight, which is where they hid in an attempt to convince the Trojans they had surrendered. As a gift to their supposed victors, the Greeks left a huge wooden horse outside of the city walls. The Trojans duly accepted the gift and hauled it inside of the city walls.

Unfortunately for the Romans, this was no generous offering, for inside of the structure lay a regiment of some forty Greek men, led by the heroic Odysseus of Homer's great poem. This band of soldiers emerged from the horse in the dead of night to be joined by their allies, who had come out of hiding. Together they caused mass devastation on the city, leading to a Greek victory and the fall of Troy.

Manlius and the Geese of Rome

The Roman historian Livy tells us the story of how Rome was saved by an excitable gaggle of geese. In about 390 BC, the Gauls staged an attack on the Roman troops outside of the city. Many soldiers lost their lives, some even jumping into the River Tiber and drowning through the weight of their armour. The survivors retreated on to the Capitol Hill, with women and children taken safely out to the outlying city districts, while the Gauls held siege.

Despite food becoming a treasured commodity for those marooned on the hill, some still gave a small portion of what they had to the flock of geese that lived there with them, since they were sacred to Juno, the wife of Jupiter. This generosity would soon work in their favour.

Eventually, the Gauls found a way to get up on to the Capitol Hill, which they approached stealthily in the dead of night. By this stage, the watchmen and guard dogs were sleeping, but as soon as the first Gaul tried to climb over the fortress walls, Juno's geese raised the alarm. The noise woke Marcus Manlius, consul of the Roman Republic, who lifted the Gaul back over the walls and alerted his fellow Romans to the attack.

Bitter fighting ensued, and the Gauls soon realized there was no way they were going to conquer the heart of the Roman city, forcing them to retreat. Each year, the Romans held a procession to commemorate the event, led by, of course, a golden goose.

Pyramus and Thisbe

In another of Ovid's teleological poems in *Metamorphoses*, he uses a tragic love story to describe why the fruits of the mulberry bush are red. In distant Babylonia, a young boy called Pyramus lived next door to a girl named Thisbe. They were fond friends as children and that soon gave way to a deep love in their teens. But their families were far from amicable and both sides disallowed the union.

The two lovers were banned from seeing one another and would communicate only through a small crack in the wall between their homes. This continued for some time, until they decided to defy their parents and meet at night outside the city walls under a mulberry bush that bore white fruit.

Thisbe arrived first, wearing a veil to hide her face. But soon after she arrived she was all of a sudden confronted by a lioness that had come to drink from the stream. In fear, she ran away and hid in a cave, dropping her veil in her haste. The lioness grabbed at the veil with its bloody jaws and soon ambled on its way. When Pyramus arrived he noticed the paw prints in the dust and became anxious. Then he saw on the ground the bloodstained veil and was convinced that Thisbe had been mauled to death.

In his grief, Pyramus took out his sword and plunged it into his side, his blood splattering the white fruit of the tree with its purple-red hue. Thisbe then returned to see her lover dying beneath the tree. With a call to the gods to immortalize their unrequited love in the colour of the berries, and a plea for the two to be buried in one tomb, she falls on his sword and dies at his side.

The keen-eyed Shakespeare fan will notice that

this myth is the clear inspiration for his great tragedy *Romeo and Juliet*, and the story of Pyramus and Thisbe is even played out in a deliberately ridiculous skit in *A Midsummer Night's Dream*.

Aeolus and the Winds

Among the many elements of nature that the Greeks and Romans personified as heroes and deities were the winds. Aeolus was the wind-keeper, and in *The Aeneid*, Juno offers him a nymph as a wife in exchange for his releasing favourable winds on to Aeneas' fleet to speed him closer to the founding of Rome.

The north wind was called Aquilo in Latin and Borealis in Greek (hence the term 'aurora borealis' for the Northern Lights), and was the violent and cold bringer of winter. He became quite smitten with the Athenian princess, Oreithyia, and, in the manner of the times, enveloped her in a dense cloud and raped her, producing four children.

The east wind was Vulturnus (Latin) or Eurus (Greek), which was famed for bringing hot, humid storms. The south wind was Auster (Latin) or Notus (Greek), and it is from this personification that we get the name for Australia, and it is from the same root as 'Austria' and – confusingly – the word 'east'. (It is thought that Italy's land mass pointing in a south-easterly direction made it easy to perceive the rising sun of the east as coming from the south.)

The west wind was Favonius (Latin) or Zephyrus (Greek). As his Latin name describes, he is a favourable wind, heralding the blossoming of spring, flowers and fruit from the west. Both he and the god Apollo had fallen in love with a young Greek prince called Hyacinth. The two vied for the boy's affections, and Apollo was eventually chosen. Favonius saw the two playing discus together, and in an uncharacteristic ire he blew the discus back, which knocked the poor boy on the head and killed him. In his grief, Apollo created the hyacinth flower from the prince's blood.

CHAPTER 9:

NORSE MYTHOLOGY

WHO WERE THE NORSE PEOPLE?

The Norsemen, or 'Northmen', belonged to the northern European countries of Scandinavia during the Viking Age from the eighth to the eleventh centuries. Known for their naval prowess, the Vikings, the explorers of the Norse world, took charge of their longboats and invaded, pillaged and settled on the lands of Europe and western Russia.

Norse mythology, which flourished before the Christianization of Scandinavia, concerned the stories of the pagan gods, heroes and kings told in Scandinavia, northern Germany and Iceland. Although not committed to writing until the eleventh century – a process that continued until the eighteenth century – the stories themselves predated this time by hundreds of years,

Because of the Vikings' influence across Europe, and because existing records of Nordic mythology lasted until relatively recently, the usage of Nordic mythology and its iconography in the modern day may surprise you.

Gods and Goddesses

The Nordics possessed a complex and colourful polytheistic religion to rival the Greeks. Like their Greek counterparts, the Nordic gods were each responsible for an important aspect of life, and each god could be offered dedications and prayer in exchange for guidance in their particular field.

The Norse gods were divided into two clans: the Aesir, warrior deities of the sky who resided in Asgard, and the Vanir, who were linked to fertility and the earth and were based in Vanaheim. The universe over which they presided was split into nine worlds, which itself was divided into three levels: the Asgard, the home of the Aesir, the Midgard 'Middle Earth', which was the home of humans, and the Niflheim, which was the home of the dead. Each of the nine worlds was connected by the World Tree, known as Yggdrasil, and each world was inhabited by a curious mix of humans, dwarves, elves, gods and other oddities. Asgard was the holiest of the nine worlds, and it could be reached via a rainbow bridge.

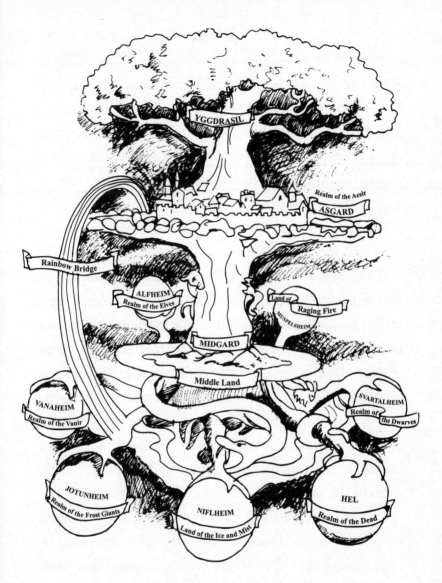

The Basis of the Norse Religion

Odin

As the father of the gods and the king of Aesir, it was Odin's duty to sit atop his throne in Asgard and (rather heroically for a god with just one eye) observe the goings on in each of the nine worlds, aided and abetted by his two ravens and two wolves, who acted as his protectors and messengers. Odin was the god of war, not to mention wisdom and poetry, and he also had strong links to the dead and the slain.

It also seems Odin was partial to alcohol, choosing to consume only wine. In fact, Odin's missing eye had been traded for a drink – although in that instance it had been for a cup full of water from the well of wisdom, from which Odin derived his immense knowledge, rather than for a large glass of Chardonnay. Regardless, Odin's one remaining eye did more than the work of two, burning as bright as the sun as he peered over the worlds. (Which is another interesting example of a myth created to help explain the movement of the sun in the sky.)

Odin's trademarks were his unfailing spear and his ring, from which another eight rings grew every ninth night. If he hadn't always been so intoxicated, Odin could probably have made himself a nice line in jewellery.

What's in a Name?

One of the most notable influences of Norse mythology is found in our names for the days of the week. Monday and Sunday were named after the moon and sun respectively, with Tuesday to Friday dedicated each to a different deity. The Nordics took the Roman names for these days and simply transposed their own corresponding god onto each day, which seems to have stuck in the Germanic languages, including English.

The table below shows where our everyday terms for every day have come from:

Day	Old Norse	Pronounced	Dedicated to
Monday	Mánadagr	mana-dagr	the moon
Tuesday	Týsdagr	tus-dagr	Tyr, god of justice
Wednesday	Óðinsdagr	othins-dagr	Odin, god of war, wisdom and poetry
Thursday	Þórsdagr	thors-dagr	Thor, god of protection and thunder
Friday	Frjádagr	frya-dagr	Freyja, goddess of love

Day	Old Norse	Pronounced	Dedicated to
Saturday	Laugardagr	laugar-dagr	Saturn, god of harvest
Sunday	Sunnudagr	sunu-dagr	the sun

Tyr

Son of Odin, Tyr was the god of war and his name derived from the same root as 'Zeus', 'Jupiter' and 'divine' – simply meaning 'god' across a range of Indo-European languages. Tyr was responsible for tying up the ferocious wolf monster, Fenrir, but at significant cost.

Fenrir had been brought to Asgard by Odin in order that he and his fellow gods could keep close watch of him. Alarmed at the animal's growth, Odin charged his son Tyr with feeding and taming the wild beast in the hope it might prevent him from destroying the Nine Worlds. Upon learning that his own fate was bound to Fenrir's, Odin decided the wolf must be tied up forever more. The gods duly attempted to tie him up with chains, but the great beast simply broke through them.

After a series of failed attempts, the gods enlisted the help of the elves, who crafted a special ribbon from the hair of a bearded lady and which, they reassured Odin, would hold the wolf down. To help gain Fenrir's trust, Tyr bravely placed his right hand in the wolf's mouth but soon found it bit clean off when Fenrir realized he was being bound by an unbreakable tie.

Thor

An enormous physical presence, Thor was the god of thunder and Odin's oldest son. He carried with him a colossal hammer with which he beat the crop (and his opponents), and the noise of which brought thunder. His enormous girdle doubled his strength and he wore a pair of iron gauntlets to help him control his hammer.

In a quest to determine whether physical power was more important than mental, Thor and Loki, a trickster and a descendent of the giants, travelled to the land of the giants to test their respective skills. Having acquired two companions en route, Thailfi and another, the four travellers finally arrived at their destination to be faced with derision – the giants thought it funny that Thor, whom they had heard so much about, was terribly tiny in size. Yet, despite their scepticism, the Giants accepted a series of challenges from Thor and his companions.

The first contest saw Loki take on one Giant in an eating contest. The table was piled high with meat, more than the giants had ever seen before. After gamely accepting the challenge, the two began to eat with the contest finally ending in a draw. However, it soon transpired that the giant had not only eaten the meat but all the bones too, which meant Loki had been defeated.

Next, their companion Thialfi challenged another giant to a race. But although Thialfi moved incredibly fast, his fellow competitor was even faster, able to reach the end of the race and turn back to meet Thialfi halfway again.

Thor then took on three of challenges of his own. The first was a drinking contest, in which he attempted to consume mead from a gigantic horn in one go. Thor drank until he thought he would explode, and yet when he looked down he saw he had only managed to drain the horn by a small amount. Second, Thor was challenged to pick up a huge grey cat. Despite using all of his might he was only able to lift one paw of the massive beast. In his third and final task, Thor challenged the giants to a fight. In the light of Thor's recent failures, the giants conceded to allow him to fight Elli, an old scullery maid, rather than themselves. However, once again Thor was defeated.

But all was not what it seemed. Despite their initial derision, the giants confessed that they were in fact intimidated by Thor's enormous strength and, as such, had decided to employ a few tricks during the contest. In the eating contest Loki had been pitted against the giant that represents fire, which eats everything in its path. Thialfi's speed race had been against the giant that represents thought, which is always faster than action. And in the challenges undertaken by Thor, he had been able to show some great feats of might, despite the tactics employed by his giant adversaries. In his drinking challenge, the bottom end of the horn was in fact being filled with water from the entire ocean, and yet Thor was able to visibly lower it. The heavy cat was, in fact, the Midgard serpent, which wraps itself around the entire world, and yet Thor had been able to shift one of its paws. And, finally, the belligerent old maid had been Old Age herself, which no one can defeat, all of which seemed to suggest that mental strength will always triumph over physical prowess.

Freyja and Frigg

Primary goddess of Vanir, Freyja is the goddess of love beauty and sexuality, the daughter of the sea god, Njord, and the giantess, Skadi, and the sister of Freyr, the god of fertility. Somewhat confusingly, according to other Germanic mythologies Freyja is also cognate with Frigg, her grandmother and the wife of Odin (see page 198). Such overlaps are too great to be ignored, and it is thought this division of one character into two distinct deities came quite late on.

As the goddess of fertility, Freyja had quite a sexual appetite and built herself something of a reputation and she was also adept at practising the Norse magic *seidr*, which she employed to manipulate the desires, health and destiny of the gods.

Having one night dreamt of owning the shiniest and most glorious piece of gold, Freyja set out the following morning to track it down. Her journey, which, unbeknownst to her, was being observed by the mischievous Loki, took Freyja to the land of the dwarves. Once she had reached her destination, Freyja descended into the dwarves' cave, and became immediately entranced by the most brilliant and intricately crafted gold necklace she had ever seen. Despite Freyja offering several riches in exchange for the necklace, the four dwarves in attendance maintained they had no need for more silver or gold; the only way they would agree to hand over the necklace was if she spent a night with each of them.

Overcome with desire for the adornment, Freyja happily consented to their wishes. Having witnessed the whole affair, Loki returned to report the scene to Odin. A little displeased on hearing the news, Odin sent

Loki to retrieve the necklace from Freyja while she slept, which he managed by first transforming himself into a fly so he could enter her palace, and then into a flea so he could bite her face so she would turn to one side and he could undo the necklace clasp.

Freyja awoke to find the necklace gone and knew immediately Loki was to blame and that he would only have done so at the behest of Odin. She begged Odin for the necklace back, to which he finally consented, but only on one condition: Freyja was to set discord, hatred and unceasing war among the mortals in Midgard; and so we have greed and desire to blame for all disharmony in the world.

Freyr

One day, when Odin was otherwise engaged, Freyr took the opportunity to sit atop his godly throne. Taking in the magnificent view of all the nine worlds, Freyr's attention was drawn to Jotunheim, the land of the giants, and, specifically, a particularly beautiful young giantess called Gerdr. Freyr became obsessed with her beauty, and yet he could tell no one of his plight – he could not risk anyone finding out he had been sitting on Odin's throne.

Concerned for Freyr's wellbeing, his family sent the servant Skirnir to find out what was wrong with his master. Freyr explained his love for the giant Gerdr and convinced Skirnir to travel to Jotunheim to woo her on his behalf. He was given Freyr's automatic giant-fighting sword and a horse that was equipped to gallop through the ring of fire that encircled Gerdr's home.

Initially, Gerdr refused the offer, even when accompanied by a bribe of gifts, commenting that a giant could never love a Vanir god, as Freyr was. Unrelenting, Skirmir resorted to force, threatening the giantess with an eternity of hunger and unrequited desire, so she graciously accepted the proposal and wed Freyr.

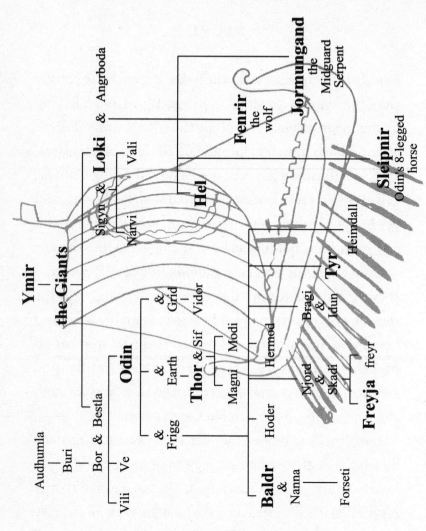

The Norse Gods' Family Tree

Hel

Daughter of Loki and the giantess Angrboda and the sister of Fenrir (the beastly wolf), Jormungand (the serpent wrapped around the world) and Sleipnir (Odin's eight-legged horse), Hel was the goddess of death, banished to the ghastly underworld by the other gods). Her ghastly appearance, with the skeleton of one side of her face fully exposed, meant she cut a terrifying figure.

As ruler of the underworld, Hel was responsible for judging the dead that come to her world (also known as Hel) and bestowing upon those that have sinned considerably in life eternal and brutal punishments. Her deadly torture chamber, from which emitted loud screams, and was made out of venomous snakes and sat atop an island of corpses in the middle of a river. Incredulously, some of the dead tried to escape from this awful chamber by means of a Naglfar – a boat made entirely out of the nail-clippings of the corpses.

To compound the awful surroundings, the entrance to Hel was guarded by monstrous guard dog named Garmr. His face dripped with the blood of those souls who had tried in vain to escape their grim fate in the underworld.

Brynhildr

After Norse people died in battle, they would be taken either to Valhalla, Odin's palace of the slain, or to Freyja's Folkvangr hall. Odin's female warriors became his Valkyries and, in exchange for immortality, they had to decide which warriors would die and live in battle. Brynhildr was one of these immortals and it was her task to pick off the loser of a battle between two kings.

Although she knew which king Odin wanted to be slain, Brynhildr decided to pick the other one, for which she was punished. Odin rescinded her immortality and set her on top of a huge mountain in the Alps surrounded her by an impenetrable ring of fire. Anyone who was able to reach her would receive her hand in marriage.

There are a few different versions of the myth, but one story involves a brave young chap called Siegfried (or Sigurd) who was the first to be able to break through the flames to reach Brynhildr. They fell in love on top of the mountain and he gave her a ring that produced reams of gold for the wearer. Before their nuptials, Siegfried visited King Gjuki and his wife Grimhild. The queen wanted Siegfried to marry her own daughter, Gudrun, and administered a potion that made him forget all about Brynhildr. Siegfried and Gudrun were then married.

Aware that poor Brynhildr was alone on top of the mountain waiting for her fiancée to return, Grimhild sent her son Gunnar to marry Brynhildr in Siegfried's place. But Gunnar was incapable of penetrating the ring of fire, leaving the onus on Siegfried to make the leap in the guise of Gunnar. Fulfilling Odin's spell, Brynhildr married the man she thought was Gunnar and returned with him.

Siegfried's wife Gudrun revealed in a heated argument with Brynhildr that it was in fact Siegfried, and not Gunnar, who had rescued her. Enraged, Brynhildr incited the younger brother of Gunnar and Gudrun to kill Siegfried in his sleep. However, it was only on his death that Brynhildr realized she had loved Siegfried all along, and so she leapt upon his burning funeral pyre and the two were sent to Hel together.

The End:
Ragnarök

Dotted throughout the tales of Norse mythology are references to a cataclysmic event that will see the end of most of the world. Known as Ragnarök ('end of rulers') and taking place at some point in the future, it will herald the end of Odin's reign, not to mention the demise of many other major gods. This terrifying apocalypse will come bearing a few tell-tale signs: three years of endless winter will kick-start proceedings and three cocks will crow – one waking the giants, another the gods, and the third raising the dead in Hel.

The sun and moon will be consumed and the stars will cease to shine, and humans will lose their morality and will be turned against one another. The ferocious wolf, Fenrir, will be released from his chains and the guard dog to Hel, Garmr, will howl at the entrance to the underworld.

The tree upon which the whole universe sits, Yggdrasil, will shake and groan, and Jormungand will writhe around, causing a great stir. Various beasts will kill various gods, and there will be huge battles in all worlds.

Eventually, fire will spread across everything and the

world will sink into the ocean – at which point the doom and gloom will cease and the world will be resurrected, fertile and fresh. Some of the gods will remain or will be reborn, and misery, greed or wickedness will have become extinct.

SELECTED BIBLIOGRAPHY

Books:

The Mythology Bible by Sarah Bartlett
(Godsfield Press, 2009)

Chinese Myths and Legends by Lianshan Chen
(Cambridge University Press, 2011)

*Mythology: The Complete Guide to Our Imagined
Worlds* by Christopher Dell (Thames and
Hudson, 2012)

The Library of Greek Mythology by Apollodorus, trans.
Robin Hard (Oxford Paperbacks, 2008)

The Oxford Companion to World Mythology by David
Leeming (Oxford University Press, 2009)

*The Greek and Roman Myths: A Guide to the Classical
Stories* by Philip Matyszak (Thames and Hudson, 2010)

Mesoamerican Mythology: A Guide to the Gods, Heroes, Rituals and Beliefs of Mexico and Central America by Kay Almere Read and Jason J. Gonzalez (OUP USA, 2002)

Websites:

Godchecker.com

Greekmythology.com

Maori.info

Pantheon.org

Wikipedia

Index

LEARN TO PLAY JACKS

I have played my fair share of jacks…and pick-up sticks, tag, hide and seek, marbles, Barbies®, a variety of board games, and anything else that would keep me entertained during long afternoons dodging my brothers. They liked to tease me, so I hid out and played games by myself.

Playing jacks is a great way to develop hand/eye coordination, no matter your age. You can do it by yourself, or with a sibling if you are feeling competitive.

> **WHAT YOU WILL NEED**
>
> Set of jacks
> (at least 10 jacks and a small ball)
>
> Flat surface, such as
> a sidewalk or a table

With all of the jacks in your hand, shake them and throw them lightly onto a flat surface. If playing on the floor or sidewalk, sit. If you use a table, it's better to stand. Your goal when disbursing the jacks is to get them near each other without having them clumped in one tangled pile.

To play, toss the ball into the air, pick up one jack in the same hand, and catch the ball before it bounces, again doing it with the same hand. Now, repeat the process, this time picking up two jacks. Continue in this manner, picking up

---

one addi
until you
the jacks
the correc
catch the b
let the oth
turn and try

TIP 👉

*bouncing the b
one or several j
before it bounces
can play by picki
for the first rou
in the second rou
4 jacks 2 times, 5
6, 7, 8, 9, and 10 j*

MIX FU

Can you believe
Murphy® Oil Soa
had to care for thei

---

provised to make their t
wooden furniture gleam
ture polish you can whip

> **WHAT YOU WILL NE**
>
> Spray bottle
>
> ½ cup olive oil
> (you can also use ano
> carrier oil, such as sweet
> or jojoba oil, but they
> probably be price
>
> ¼ cup lemon juic
>
> Clean cloths

Respray the cloth as n
polishing in circles. Be

Yields 3/4 cup

I've been knitting f
the wool from a she
a trip back home, I

of The Weekend Weaver (weekendweaver.com). Wendy and her fellow spinners, Joan Hawkins and Peggy Coffey, opened my eyes, and I have another homespun hobby to fit into my already-crowded crafting schedule.

WHAT YOU WILL NEED

Roving or Cloud

Flyer and bobbin spinning wheel

Scrap yarn

Ball winder

2 containers, such as boxes or clean trash bins

Knitting noddy

Yarn swift

Start with wool **roving** (raw fiber that's been cleaned, collected, and brushed in one direction to produce long tufts of fiber) or **cloud** (fiber that's been cleaned and collected in large, unbrushed clumps) in the fiber and color of your choice (wool, preferably low in lanolin, is always classic and you can use undyed or dyed fibers). Go with the best fiber you can afford. Even though your yarn results may not be perfect your first time, you'll have a much happier experience when you work with good material.

Sit in a chair in front of a spinning wheel with your roving/cloud at your side. Tie a lead string (a piece of scrap yarn) to the bobbin. Notice the hooks on the flyer on the side of the bobbin? Wrap the lead string around the hook closest to you, and pull the loose end through the hole in front of the flyer and bobbin assembly.

You are ready to spin, which involves drafting and then spinning

your fibers into yarn. Drafting is the process of pulling your fibers apart so you can spin them on the wheel. Roving fibers are densely packed together, so it's important to stagger and thin out the fibers if you want a thin ply during drafting. Before you it to the spinning wheel, pull a chunk of roving/cloud from your pile. If you are using roving, gently pull apart your piece from both ends.

Slowly press down on the spinning wheel's pedal and practice treadling consistently in one direction. You want all of your fiber to be drafted in one direction (S twist or Z twist) before you spin two or more plies together in the opposite direction.

Hold the lead string and one end of your roving/cloud together in your left hand and use your right hand to feed the raw fiber and control tension as you spin. Start treadling slowly. The raw fiber will stick to the lead string and start spinning into a ply collected on the wheel's bobbin. Keeping the spinning action in front of your left hand, continue feeding fiber from your right hand to your left. Yarn will start to collect on the bobbin. When it starts to get bulky on the bobbin, stop treadling and move the yarn from the front hook to the next one. Keep an eye on your bobbin as you draft and move the yarn from hook to hook as necessary.

When you fill a bobbin, stop spinning, cut the yarn, and put the bobbin aside and let the yarn rest for 24 hours. Tie off skein and wash.

If you have more than one bobbin, place the single-spun bobbins on a **lazy kate** (a device that allows bobbins to spin independently of each other without tangling) and feed the strands into the spinning wheel on a third bobbin in an opposite direction than you spun the singles. For instance, spin in a clockwise direction and ply in a counterclockwise direction. Hold the two strands in your left hand, with a couple of fingers separating them. Use your right hand to keep the strands untangled with a bit of tension. Spin the two yarns onto a bobbin, again moving the yarn on the hook from the front to the back hook as the bobbin fills up. Always spin the yarn in front of your left hand to avoid tight curly strands. The plied yarn can be transferred from the bobbin to the niddy noddy to form a skein.

All hand spun has to be washed to set the twist. Soak the skein in cool water. For wool, let it sit for least 20 minutes. Change the dirty water. Then wash with mild detergent by hand, gently squeezing skein. Rinse, but do not agitate, in cool water. Hang over a rounded plastic hanger to drip dry over a tub. Weight the skeins with a wet towel, hanging over the loop. Let it all dry together. Now you are ready to use the swift and the ball winder. The two-ply is for knitting.

When you are ready to use your skein, put it on a yarn swift and wind it on a ball winder. Drape your skein over the yarn swift, removing any ties or knots in the yarn. Push up the yarn swift, much like opening an umbrella, until the skein is firmly in place. Secure the yarn swift at this tension. Take an end of the skein and feed it through a ball winder, which should be clamped to a table next to the swift. Start cranking the winder, which will pull the yarn from the skein on the swift to the winder. When done, pull your ball up and off the winder. Your homespun yarn is ready to use.

SPIN A YARN (OR TALL TALE)

What pioneers lacked in electronic entertainment, they made up with telling stories. The oral tradition had quite a different meaning back then. Families gathered around the stove after dinner and shared fantastical stories, tall tales, and familiar fables. Public-speaking skills were honed in private and, from an early age, a prairie gal could spin a yarn to delight the masses or frighten her kin. Don't you want to scare the bejeezus out of a coworker or woo a suitor with a perfectly delivered yarn?

Before you open your mouth, prepare. Even the most comfortable, seemingly off-the-cuff speaker plots out her comments in advance. Study other raconteurs

---

WHAT YOU WILL NEED

Advance planning

Pen and paper

Mirror

A steady voice

Moxie

you admire—their voice, timing, delivery, gestures. Analyzing individual components can give you ideas for your own yarn. Write out your tale, and memorize key passages or the entire thing. Practice your story out loud in front of a mirror. If you want to introduce voices for various characters, make sure they are distinctive and different from each other. For example, a girl with a lisp and a German accent would be a nice foil to a booming, pompous man.

As for the story, draft it out on paper, so you can work on key areas: foreshadowing, building to a climax, a strong but unexpected punch line. Commit certain phrases to memory but outline the entire tale.

As you speak, take stock of your pace. If it sounds hurried to

WIN A SPELLING BEE

Back in the day, I was a regular on the competitive spelling circuit, and I'm lending my skills to help you with some spelling tips, whether you're at the microphone or in front of the computer.

When you come across a word you don't know, write it out. The act of writing out each letter will help you picture the word in your head.

Next, visualize the word. Break it into individual syllables. Look for prefixes, suffixes, and roots, all of which offer clues as to the word's spelling and meaning.

Keep a running list of words you don't know or can't spell. Whenever you have a few minutes, review the list. Use each word in a sentence.

Developing memory aids helps you become a better speller. Coming up with clever memory tricks—such as the princi*pal* is your *pal*—sticks with you when it comes time to spell a word.

While fancy spellcheck functions in computers can catch a word that is misspelled, they cannot discern between the right word and the wrong one. For example, if you "right the write word," a spellcheck won't figure out that you meant "write the right word."

you, it is. Take a breath and slow your pace. Trust that your audience will stick with you. That said, don't let the story go on too long or people will get distracted or lose interest. Pepper your story with a few choice details. If you hear laughter or gasps, pause for dramatic effect (this is a great time to take a swig of water).

Stay on track and resist the urge to segue into rambling side stories. Keep your energy and animation high: If you get tired of talking, using accents, or gesturing, chances are your listeners will pick up on it. Save up your energy and let it build as you work toward your yarn's conclusion. When you've finished your story, proclaim "The End!" and bow. You deserve it. Bask in the glow of your admirers (and the fireplace).

LAY A FIRE

I like fire—campfires, fireplaces, gas stoves, a lit match—and as long as it's in a controlled environment, I find fire magical and comforting. It takes me back to telling tall tales and secrets around the campfire, caroling around the hearth, warming my feet next to the wood-burning stove. Here's how to create a safe fire, be it in or out of doors.

Scout out a location for your fire pit, well away from low-hanging branches, dry brush, and your tent or homestead. (Note: Make sure it is legal to build a fire in your location.) The ground should be dry

WHAT YOU WILL NEED

If working outside:
Spade or shovel

If working outside:
Large stones, optional
(the number of stones will
be determined by the desired
size of the fire pit)

Tinder, such as dry brush,
pine needles, and
crumpled newspaper

Kindling, such as small twigs,
sticks, and twisted newspaper

Dry logs, both large and small

If working outside,
2 buckets of sand or water

Fire starter,
such as matches or a lighter

Note: If you are indoors, you can
skip over creating a fire pit and
jump straight to laying your fire.
This works for fireplaces and
wood-burning stoves. Start small
and avoid a blaze; you can always
add wood after the fire gets going.

and shielded from the wind. With the edge of a spade or shovel, mark out a circular pit about two feet in diameter. Dig four inches out of your pit. Remove any flammable materials: live or dead grass, sticks, leaves, needles and the like (note that this all can be used in your fire). Pack large stones, if available, around the edge of your pit. Your pit is prepped.

In addition to a match or lighter, you'll need three kinds of material for your fire: tinder (dry brush, pine needles, wood shavings, birds' nests, and the like); kindling (small twigs and branches); and logs, as dry as possible. Gather as many of these materials before you start your fire, so you can keep it stoked without running low on fuel. Store your materials well away from your fire pit.

There are several ways to lay a fire, but the guiding principle is to create ventilation space between and under your layers. I like to as-

semble a base of tinder in a small pile. I then angle kindling around the pile, so it forms a loose teepee or lean-to. This also serves to protect the kindling from the wind. You can also layer kindling loosely over the tinder.

Before lighting your fire outside, fill two buckets with water or sand and keep them nearby, should you need to put out your fire quickly.

With a hand blocking the wind, strike your match and carefully light the edges of the tinder. Blow gently on the flame, toward the rest of the tinder. As the fire catches and grows, add more kindling. Once you have a small fire going, slowly add larger wood and stoke it periodically to maintain it. To avoid sparks and embers, add new logs carefully. If you can find them, pinecones add a fragrant touch to the fire.

As you did when first laying your fire, make sure there is space between logs to ensure ventilation (placing logs on the fire in a lattice configuration or at an angle is a good way to do this). Adding too many logs at once can smother your fire.

To put out your fire, sprinkle water or sand on the embers. Stir the embers to spread the water. When there is no more steam, the fire is out.

Off the reel: immediately.
"When the fire started to spread, Annabelle grabbed her prized possessions and left right off the reel."

PRACTICE THE ART OF COURTSHIP

I think I'm a modern gal. However, when it comes to dating, I'm decidedly old-fashioned. I prefer boys to ask me out, and I wait for them to make the first move, be it holding my hand or holding the door. But it's difficult to know when to be traditional and when to just be yourself without strategy or guile.

WHAT YOU WILL NEED

Restraint

Subtlety

Soft clothes, hair, and makeup

When you take notice of a young man, make eye contact. Shy glances, looking away, and then looking him in the eye will convey your interest without being too forward. When he approaches you—which he will, trust me—let him engage you in conversation. While it's easy to take the conversational reins, remain curious about what he's going to say and leave him room to direct the talk.

When he is near, take the opportunity to touch his arm, particularly if you are making a point or joking with him. Warm and receptive body language is an excellent way to convey your interest without appearing to be the town hussy.

While some may think men are intimidated by a modern working gal, the truth is that they love it when you have a full life. So keep your days

THE MODERN PRAIRIE GAL WAY

While it may seem near to impossible to meet eligible men in these modern times, think about how challenging it was for gals on the open range. Pickins were slim, as there probably weren't a lot of unattached men from which to choose, especially in the surrounding towns. But as prairie gals are wont to do, they made do.

Today, there are loads of opportunities to meet nice young men from good families. Try your hand at old-fashioned flirting in a variety of places: the grocery store, a coffee shop, on the bus, anywhere and everywhere. Be strategic: On the subway, sit next to strapping men who are ringless, or at a bustling café, ask a boy if you can share his table. The great thing about these modern times is that you won't be taken for a "cherry," old-fashioned slang for a vulgar young woman. But you might just get taken out for a night on the town.

rich and active. Work him around your chores; don't forgo them.

And while this may smack of game playing, keep your contact old-fashioned, at least at first. That is, keep your telephone and e-mail contact minimal and opt for meeting in person. It's far too easy to adopt a sense of familiarity with someone over the phone and online, and you can get ahead of yourself if you don't also spend ample time in each other's company getting to know each other.

And that brings me to pacing. Go slow. Don't let a beau's attentions go to your head so that you make yourself available every night. You still need to get to know each other. While a young man might come on like a house on fire, once he's reeled you in, he might take you for granted or lose interest if you display too much interest. You don't want to scare him back to his own homestead. Give a man space to come to you, to bring something to the table, to *win* you. Let him be a man, and enjoy being a girl.

Being a girl means expecting gentlemanly behavior. Let him call on you, open doors for you, and ask you out. Being a girl also means embracing your feminine side. That doesn't mean that you have to don petticoats and corsets, but do play up your best features, wear soft clothes, hair, and makeup.

He'll be yours by the time the ice cream social rolls around.

TRIM A CHRISTMAS TREE WITH HAND-STRUNG GARLAND

Christmas holds a special place in my heart and not just because of the gift giving. I love the smell of fresh pine, so therefore I adore real Christmas trees. As the years have gone by, I've seen my parents add a random but meaningful ornament here and there, and I've taken on the tradition. I eschew artificial trees and decoration themes. I much prefer the heartfelt jumble of ornaments collected through-out the years, backlit by large multicolored bulbs and bubble lights. While modest, these ornaments are among my most treasured heirlooms.

And rather than sprinkle tinsel all over the tree, I opt for more, shall we say, *organic* decorations. A popcorn-and-cranberry garland is just the rustic prairie touch you need for a really charming tree and holiday. And for a gift to your surroundings, consider draping the trees outside your window with garlands as well. They will attract all sorts of birds to your yard, making your garlands a gift you'll both give and receive.

WHAT YOU WILL NEED

Popcorn
(see p. 47 for information on
popping corn)

Cranberries

Large sewing needle

White thread
(any kind will do)

Pop several bowls of popcorn and place them near a large bowl of cranberries.

Thread your needle with any sort of plain cotton or polyester thread, and knot both ends together. You will string five feet of cranberries and popcorn at a time, so you'll need ten feet of thread if you knot the ends.

Run a needle through a cranberry and pull it to near the end of your thread, tie a knot around the berry by bringing the end of the thread up and over the cranberry, knotting the thread just above the berry. Now it's time to string your garland. I like a high popcorn-to-cranberry ratio, meaning I string about 10 pieces of popcorn to every one cranberry. Your preference may be different. Whatever the case, thread through the center of each berry and the meatiest part of the popcorn. If the corn cracks, set it aside to snack on later.

TIP *It's easiest to sit at a table while doing this, but you can be anywhere. Just be advised that your hands will become stained from the berries, so if you aren't careful, you could stain your clothes or upholstery.*

When you have about six inches of thread left, tie off your garland by knotting around a cranberry in the same manner as you started. Taking care not to tangle your garland, carefully carry it to the tree and lay it gently on the boughs. Continue making garlands until you have draped your tree to your satisfaction.

THE MODERN PRAIRIE GAL WAY

When I think of early settlers delighting over a stick of peppermint and a handknit scarf on Christmas morning, I feel downright spoiled but also a bit put out. I long for the days when one gift meant the world, even if it cost next to nothing. It was about the thought and love that went into the gift. For a prairie-worthy holiday that's truly warm and meaningful, consider adding a few traditional or primitive touches around your home to create a heartfelt and festive experience.

* Wrap a quilt around the bottom of your Christmas tree.
* Wrap gifts with kraft paper and twine, adorning them with fresh branches and pinecones.
* Make your own ornaments: Weave a ribbon around a pinecone, make an interlocking paper chain out of construction paper.
* Hang real stockings from your mantel.

ICE CREAM SOCIAL

I think ice cream socials have always been a big hit because eating ice cream is sure to put even the crabbiest person in a good mood and turn the most antisocial soul into a social butterfly. Prairie gals had to break into the icehouse if they wanted to make ice cream in the summer, but you can enjoy the creamy treat year-round. Ice cream parlors sprouted up all over the country in the early 20th century, and while we've come a long way in terms of refrigeration, why not set up shop in your home and invite a few folks over for an honest-to-goodness ice cream social?

See p. 37 for instructions on making homemade ice cream. Start with vanilla as your base flavor, and provide a passel of toppings, including:

* Hot fudge (put it on the stove and let it simmer on the lowest setting)
* Chocolate sauce
* Butterscotch
* Caramel

* Fruit, including berries, bananas, and cherries
* Nuts (keep these away from other ingredients, in the event a guest has an allergy)
* Granola
* Crumbled candy bars
* Crushed peppermint sticks

Add flavoring to your ice cream while you are making it. Consider adding some chocolate syrup to make a chocolate ice cream. Yum.

Provide sugar and cake cones (or make your own waffle cones if you have a waffle iron), along with dishes and spoons, if your guests prefer a sundae. Set ice cream scoops nearby in cups of warm water (which will help to soften the ice cream when scooping), and invite your guests to dig in. For a fun touch, create recipe cards, listing several classic and unusual combinations for guests to consider when building their ice cream treat. For instance, I enjoy a makeshift butter pecan: Add butterscotch and crushed pecans to the top of your scoop of vanilla. Or add shredded coconut, granola, and banana over vanilla for a tropical treat. Crumble up shredded peppermint sticks and sprinkle it over the top of a hot fudge and chocolate ice cream sundae.

Bring out the ice cream when you are ready to serve up your sundaes and cones. If you anticipate the party going on for a while, you can keep the ice cream in coolers or ice buckets.

And when guests get ready to roll out, hand them each a serious ice cream scoop or fancy topping so they can enjoy a one-person ice cream social in the comfort of their own homes.

Cold as a wagon tire: dead.
*"Pa found the fox cold as a wagon tire so they wouldn't
have to worry about it stealing any more chickens."*

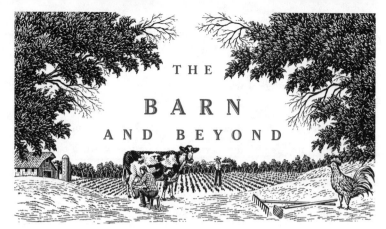

THE
BARN
AND BEYOND

Like they do any prairie girl, barns send me over the moon. I can still smell the stale hay of Grandpa's ramshackle barn. It smelled inviting and sort of sweet, and as a child, my brothers and I would swing off of thick ropes into the hay, a soft but scratchy dismount.

I spent a lot of time out of doors as a kid. My brothers and I set up obstacle courses in the shed with overturned bushel baskets and raced Hot Wheels® against a cast-iron John Deere™ miniature tractor. Later, we moved on to other more dangerous pursuits. John broke his arm after I dared him to jump off the roof of the shed, and Chris set up his own rappelling system on the side of my grandparents' border house.

But there was too much work to be done to get into much trouble. Although we didn't have livestock to care for, we did have vegetables to plant and harvest, firewood to collect and split, wild asparagus and wildflowers to gather. Whether I was digging up potatoes or shucking lima beans, I felt connected to my family and the earth. I felt at peace.

Don't get me wrong—I was drawn to the more rambunctious activities, curious about everything new. But like prairie gals before me, I feel a deep satisfaction in working with my hands and pride in a job well done. I find few things better than slipping between cool sheets at the end of a day of vigorous work, muscles sore and mind clear. And as I slip off into an untroubled slumber, I look forward to the chores, tasks, and handicrafts that await me upon waking.

GO ICE FISHING

It gets cold out there in the wilderness. Critters scatter, and you might deplete your stores of grains, preserves, and the like. Or maybe you just want the taste of fresh fish alongside your staples. Whatever the case, it's handy to know how to catch a fish even if the bay or lake is frozen over. Ice fishing is popular in areas that have long, cold winters and bodies of waters, such as Minnesota and Alaska. But it can be done anywhere, as long as the ice is thick enough to support you and whatever gear you drag along with you. But beware—you can't just head out onto a frozen lake like an original pioneer fisherwoman. Check local regulations regarding safety and permits so you don't find yourself in hot water.

WHAT YOU WILL NEED

Safety equipment and
warm clothing

Ice auger or a drill with
a sharp blade

Ice dipper

Rod, reel, and tackle
(including colorful lures, spoons,
bait, hooks, bobbers)

Chair or bucket to sit on

Trash bag for fish and litter

First, locate a body of water with thick frozen ice. Ice should be at least four inches thick to support your weight and twelve inches to support structures or vehicles. The color should be crystal and white; cloudy or gray ice is not as strong. Check thickness often, as the thickness of ice near shore may be much greater than farther out.

To that end, it is wise to carry a sturdy pole horizontally with you as you walk, since if you fall through the ice, the pole can support you as you work your way out. Wear a life preserver, carry a long rope, and for goodness sake, dress for warmth and wear loads of layers.

Scout out a suitable location. Fish go where their food goes, and in the winter, smaller prey tend to stay closer to shore and near nutrient-rich areas, such as reed deposits and small shelves. The point of a bay, for example, is a great place to set up shop. Clear snow from your chosen fishing hole. With an ice auger (a corkscrew-like tool that lets you bore holes in the ice), drill, chisel, spade, or saw, cut a circular or rectangular hole in the ice. Remove chunks of ice with an ice dipper, which often looks like a large slotted spoon on a long stick. Pull up the loose ice with it and set it to the side of your hole.

While there are different ways to fish, let's focus on fishing with a rod, reel, and lure.

Add small, colorful lures to a light fishing line and rod. Tie a flashy fishing spoon, a lure that is thin, flat, and curved with a hook on the end, to the end of your line (when you drop your line in the water, the spoon will take the slack out of your line and attract attention). Small quantities of bait (worms, minnows, crawlers, etc.) can improve your odds as well. Now is not the time to be squeamish; spear the bait on your hook and put it in the water. (If you really want to test your prairie mettle, my Canadian friend Rob Sorensen recommends warming the bait as a further incentive for the fish. The old-school way to do this is to keep the worm inside your lower lip until you are ready to bait your hook. Don't worry—no one will judge you if you draw the line here.)

Fish have slow metabolisms in cold water, so they move slower and with more subtlety. Because of this, you should drop your line in the water and jig (that is, wiggle or jerk) it slowly and pause frequently to give the fish a chance to bite. A bobber at the top of your line will help determine if you've got a bite. Check your rod and line frequently to make sure both are free of ice. If your first hole doesn't yield fruit, er, fish, after a short while, make another hole and try again. It may take some trial and error with your holes until you hit upon a rich fishing hole.

When you do get a bite, pull up on the rod to set the hook and reel it in. After your hard day of fishing, let someone else clean the fish, then enjoy your fresh catch with your winter staples. Bring along a bucket to sit on while you fish and to transport your catch when you head for shore.

TIP *If you take to ice fishing, you may want to consider toting a shelter of some kind along with you. Some fish houses can be quite elaborate, others a simple hut or tent.*

PAN FOR GOLD

Ah, gold. I've always been attracted to all things shiny, and pioneers were no different. They rushed to the West to strike it rich. Some were more successful than others, but at least they got to wade in streams and rivers while they worked the sieve.

I've never panned for gold myself, but during one memo-

Pull foot:
to leave in a hurry.
"Once she found gold in the stream, Ella pulled foot and headed home to show the nuggets to her ma."

rable family vacation to Michigan's Upper Peninsula, we all engaged in the wholesome activity of wading in the Eagle River and looking for copper. Since we didn't have a covered wagon, we loaded up our five-pound chunk of copper into the back of the family van. Back at the homestead, we used it as a doorstop. Since you can pan for rocks in many geographic areas, check online for mineral-rich streams and riverbeds. My brother Chris enjoys mining the streams and exploring abandoned mines near his home in Georgia, and he was extremely helpful in showing me the proper panning technique.

WHAT YOU WILL NEED

Small shovel

12-inch-round gold pan
(steel or plastic pan with a lip)

Handful of BBs or steel shot

Jar

Funnel

Tweezers

Look for areas likely to yield gold, namely areas of exposed bedrock in rivers or streams. This way, you won't have to sift through clay, sand, silt, and other debris that might be covering up minerals. Gold has a greater gravity than other materials, so it sinks to the bottom of sand and gravel, as well as to the bottom of your pan. The presence of black sand is a good indicator that gold is near, so if you are panning and everything's coming up white, gray, or brown, it's best to move along.

Wade out into the water and remove as much sediment (clay, sand, silt, stones) as you can from the area where you want to pan. You

should eventually hit rocks and stones. Remove them as well until you hit bedrock, the solid rock layer. Depths for these layers can vary, so don't despair, just keep digging. When you hit bedrock, shovel six to twelve inches of gravel into a flat, round pan until the pan is half full (or half empty, depending on how you look at it!).

Once you have gravel in your pan, the fun really begins. Fill the rest of the pan with water and stir the contents around with your finger, carefully pouring out the muddy water. You are getting rid of dirt and silt while cleaning what's left in the pan.

TIP *Throw a handful of BBs in your pan. They will sink to the bottom of your pan, along with your gold. If you manage to keep the BBs in your pan while rapid panning, you'll also be sure of keeping your gold in there as well.*

Place your hands at the nine and three o'clock positions (see the illustration above) and, with one inch of water covering the sand and gravel, gently swirl the contents 15 to 20 times. Avoid sloshing water over the pan edge.

*Rock the pan from side to side while simultaneously tipping the pan away from you, allowing the water to spill out of the pan, as shown in the illustration on p. 161. The wave action will move the coarser material to the top of the pan and some of the bigger gravel and debris will actually slosh out.

With the pan level, immerse it in water until the contents are covered by an inch of water. Rock—do not swirl—your pan side to side while it's underwater. This will help any gold settle to the bottom.

Level the pan with an inch of water in it and repeat the steps from * until only a few tablespoons are left in your pan. Use less water this time as you have less material remaining in your pan. You should be able to see black sand, a good indication of gold!

When there is very little material remaining and what does remain looks like black sand, quartz, and maybe even gold, carefully tilt the pan away from you, pushing any remaining sand or quartz over the lip of your pan with your thumb or hand. I recommend having the pan just out of the water. Level the pan and repeat this tilting until most of the quartz and sand have been removed and separated from the gold and the BBs. Wash the remaining gold and sand into a jar using a funnel and examine it later.

When you are ready to separate out your gold, put it into a pan with the rest of the black sand and anything else remaining. Pour just enough water to cover your sand and gold. Keeping your pan level, swirl slowly and evenly. Sand should start separating itself from heavier black sand, which should be followed by even heavier gold. Pick out any gold flecks with tweezers.

WHITTLE

While I appreciate elaborate woodworking, I've always been drawn to more primitive pieces. I dig a rustic pine pie safe with punched tin doors over fancy-pants carved chairs with silk upholstered seats. I like things that are utilitarian, perhaps with a bit of embellishment. It's no wonder I'm crazy for carved duck decoys and small whittled items. My grandfather used to carve red cardinals and we'd stick them on the end of our split-rail fence. My uncle, Greg Hamlin, has continued the tradition of woodworking, and I turned to him for some instruction on how to carve my own bird without doing serious injury to myself.

Decide what you want to whittle. Since you are a beginner, don't worry about making your bird three-dimensional. Find a silhouette of a bird (such as a cardinal or sandpiper) or other easy shape. Using a pencil, lightly draw it on your piece of wood (basswood, a soft wood with a straight grain, is a good choice). Modify your shape as you go.

Open up your pocketknife and hold the handle, not the blade. Sit at a table, which will catch your shavings and wood pieces, as well as protect your body.

A good technique for handling your knife is to hold it in your dominant hand. As you cut, hold onto your wood with the other hand and push the blade along the wood with the thumb on your

WHAT YOU WILL NEED

2 by 4 by 12-inch piece of basswood or another soft wood (such as pine)

Pencil

Pocketknife with at least one sharp blade

100- or 150-grit sandpaper

½ pint oil-based primer, like Rust-Oleum® (optional)

½ pint oil-based paint, like Rust-Oleum (optional)

Small foam brushes (optional)

Oil-based artist's paint (optional)

Horsehair paintbrush(es) (optional)

Old newspapers

1 pint Minwax® Wood Finish™, with wood stain of your choice (optional)

Small foam brush (optional)

Drill (optional)

Wood glue (optional)

Two small round sticks (optional)

Small piece of driftwood or stump (optional)

nondominant hand. This will give you more control than just trying to carve using one hand. Always cut away from your body.

Make your first cut at a shallow angle. This is a good way to gauge the softness of your wood. If you have to remove a lot of wood and it's soft, go ahead and make some long, deep cuts. If it's harder than you expected, just continue to whittle using small, shallow strokes. Regardless, start by getting rid of square corners and the largest unnecessary sections of the wood. Try to envision your three-dimensional bird inside the cut stock of the wood, but only work in two dimensions until you have the whole outline of your bird carved. As you hone in on your bird silhouette, make smaller and more refined cuts along your pencil lines.

When you have whittled out the flat shape of your bird, round the edges with small, shallow cuts. Sand the wood with 100- or 150-grit sandpaper to smooth out your creation.

If you want a more finished look, use a foam brush, paint a coat of oil-based primer, such as one by Rust-Oleum, all over your carving. With oil-based enamel paint (Rust-Oleum also makes good paints for this) that match the natural colors of your bird, paint your bird with a base coat and allow it to dry. Add detail, such as feathers and wings, with different paints and allow it to dry.

If you want to keep your bird natural, protect the wood and deepen the color by brushing Minwax (a stain and sealant) over your work with a small foam brush. Cover your table with old newspapers to protect the surface.

To display your bird, drill two small holes in the bottom of your bird. Squirt a drop of wood glue into each hole then insert two round sticks for legs into your bird. Attach it to a base by similarly drilling and gluing the legs to a small branch, piece of driftwood, or stump.

TIP *Besides a bird, other basic shapes suitable for your first whittling project include a ship, train, or favorite flower or animal. As you get more adept, consider whittling your own Christmas ornament or dowels for a shoe rack or jewelry display.*

MILK A COW

I lived in a ranch-style house that my parents built down the road from my grandparents' farmhouse. In between the two homes were a shed and an abandoned, rundown barn that cows once called home. I just called it a low-budget playground. But back in his day, my dad, true to our prairie roots, went into that very same barn and milked the farm's one cow to have milk for the family and to sell to the local creamery. He taught me all I needed to know about milking a cow.

WHAT YOU WILL NEED

Dairy cow

Stool

Sterile bucket (place it
in boiling water before using)

Double boiler

2 large pots

Jars

If your dairy cow isn't secured, place her in a stanchion, which is a yoke-like object that closes over the cow's neck to prevent her from turning her head to check out what you're doing. To make sure the cow cooperates with you, talk softly and treat her gently during the process.

Sit on a low stool next to the cow, and place a bucket under the udder. Grab the teat closest to you between your thumb and forefinger. Now squeeze your second, third, and fourth fingers in a row, rolling your fingers and pulling down at the same time. You are pushing milk down to the opening and into the bucket. Repeat the process with the second teat and your other hand. Continue milking, alternating hands and teats and making sure that you get milk into your bucket.

When the first two teats are fully milked, move onto the other two on the other side of the cow, and repeat the process. When your bucket gets full, replace it

Some pumpkins:
someone or
something impressive.
*"Isla thought her
calf was some pumpkins."*

with another bucket or pour your new milk into a large milk can or receptacle. Do not drink your milk without pasteurizing it. You can send it to a pasteurizing plant or do it yourself. To pasteurize it, place raw milk in a double boiler. Bring a pot of water to a boil and place the double boiler in the pot. Heat your milk to 161.5°F and hold it there for at least 15 seconds, stirring constantly. Place your double boiler full of milk in a new pot full of cold water to rapidly cool the milk. When it reaches 130°F, replace the cold water with ice water. Stir occasionally. When the milk reaches 40°F, pour into glass jars, seal, and refrig-

erate. Your milk should keep for two to three weeks.

TIP *Milk your cow twice a day if possible. As long as it eats grass, it will produce a lot of milk.*

GROOM AND SADDLE A HORSE

While I've always longed for a pony, I've never been astride a horse. I intended to take lessons but haven't gotten around to it quite yet. I think this is due to a bad spill my mother once took when she rented a horse for my brother's birthday party. She thought it would go over big, but Mom's the one who went over…the side of the horse.

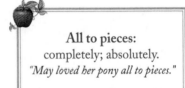

However traumatic the memory, I love the culture of horses and the smell of a worn saddle. But like a self-respecting prairie girl, I still dream of my pony—

All to pieces:
completely; absolutely.
"May loved her pony all to pieces."

rubbing it down, feeding it carrots, and maybe even riding it. I recently spent some time talking with Paula Nasiatka, a National Park Service ranger and owner of an Arabian, on how to properly care for a horse.

GROOMING

Before you attempt to groom a horse, it is necessary to think as they do. Because horses have a reputation for being skittish, anticipate problems, use slow, steady movements, and talk in a calm voice when grooming the animal.

When approaching the horse, make eye contact and talk to it. Slowly walk up at a 30-degree angle so it can see you (horses' eyes are

WHAT YOU WILL NEED

Hoof pick

Curry comb and brush

Mane comb or brush

Mane-and tail-shampoo

Mane-and-tail conditioner

Water

Bucket

very wide spaced and they can see you better at an angle). Put a halter on the horse and use the lead rope to take it to a hitching rail.

Start by cleaning the hooves. Spread your legs and face toward the horse's rear. Start with the front right leg. Run your hand down the horse's leg. When your hand travels below its knee, the horse should bend its leg. Using a hoof pick, pick out mud, pebbles, and any clumps of dirt.

Ideally, horses should be groomed every few days if they are kept outside. If they are kept in a stall, groom them every two days. There are several types of brushes for grooming (a fine one for the muzzle, thicker ones for the back, body, and legs, for example).

With a curry brush and a firm, steady hand, brush in a circular motion on the horse's back and belly to remove dirt and dried sweat. Next, brush in the direction of hair growth.

Now move to the horse's mane. With a mane comb or brush, comb from root to end slowly, taking care not to pull on a snag. Work out any tangles with a comb. If you have time, wash the mane with mane-and-tail shampoo and a bucket of warm water, taking care not to get shampoo in the horse's eyes. The slickness of the shampoo and water will help detangle the hair. Rinse well. Follow up in the same manner with a conditioner, again rinsing thoroughly. Do not shampoo a horse in colder weather, unless it is sheltered in a warm stable.

TIP ☞　 *Take extra care grooming any areas that will have contact with the saddle. There's not much worse for a horse than to have something pricking it under the saddle. Grooming is a wonderful opportunity to connect with your horse. Talk as you brush the animal.*

SADDLING

WHAT YOU WILL NEED

Saddle pad

Saddle

Halter and lead rope

Lunge line

Lunge whip

Bridle

Make sure you have a saddle that fits your horse first and you second. Horses can get crippled or lame with an ill-fitting saddle. The saddle should fit comfortably on its back and not be too large or small. Check with a horse trainer if you're unsure about fitting a saddle. Approach the horse from the side at a 30-degree angle. Walk slowly and refrain from any sudden movements. Check that the underside of the saddle pad is free from briars. Lay a clean, thick, and fluffy saddle pad on its back. Start up high at the withers (the ridge between the shoulders of the horse) and then pull the pad down to where you want it. This way, it lies with the direction of the horse's hair growth.

Use your hand to feel where
the horse's shoulder blade is and
place the saddle on the horse's
back, so that the front of the
saddle is not interfering with the
shoulder's movement in any way.
There should be a hand width

One-horse:
small, limited, inferior.
*"I need to get out of this one-horse
town," Jillian thought to herself
when she couldn't find the right
poplin for her petticoat.*

between the edge of the shoulder and the front of the saddle.

As you prepare to cinch the saddle, remember to treat the horse
like you want to be treated. Place your hand under the saddle horn to
see that you are leaving a bit of breathing space in front. The saddle
pad should be high up against the saddle and the saddle should
be firmly in place (you don't want it to slip or move while riding).
Pull the cinch strap once it is through the D-ring—don't yank—to
tighten slowly. Cinch to what you think is tight. Right before you get
on, recheck the cinch because the horse might have exhaled and
made it looser.

Unclip the halter and place it around the horse's neck, leaving it
fairly loose. It should be secured but not uncomfortable. Before bri-
dling, it's a good idea to lunge your horse to loosen up its muscles
and see the horse's form. Clip a lunge line to the halter ring behind
the horse's chin and remove the lead rope before lunging. Holding the
other end of the lunge line, rotate the line in a circle in the same direction as you want the horse to go. Use a lunge whip to help reinforce

your walk, trot, and canter commands. Switch directions and lunge your horse in the opposite direction for the same amount of time.

Now place the bit in the horse's mouth. To do this, tuck your left index finger in the side of the mouth and the horse should willingly open up. Guide the bit in and let the horse chew on it. Then, with your right arm, bring the bridle over the ears, doing the right ear first. Fasten the bridle under the chin with the strap that comes down from

behind the ears. Also fasten it above the nose. Make sure the bridle is snug and then re-check your cinch. It fits properly when you can tightly slide a hand underneath it. You can then remove the halter and leave it at the hitching rail.

You're almost ready to ride. *Almost.*

Don't get on the horse immediately. Walk the horse for 20 to 30 feet while leading it by the reins. Doing this allows you to observe whether the horse seems to have any problems with the saddle, and it allows the horse time to get comfortable and stretch.

Muck Out a Stall

Mucking out a stall may not be the most genteel part of prairie life, but it is an everyday chore for any horse owner. If the horse is stabled

WHAT YOU WILL NEED

Stall/muck rake

Wheelbarrow

inside, put down rubber mats and add wood shavings or grindings on top of them. Every day you have to clean out the stall, as horses "do their business" there, unless they are "indoor/outdoor" animals.

Using a muck rake, scoop up manure and place it in a wheelbarrow to dump elsewhere (preferably downwind of the stable and the homestead). Replace the shavings in the stall every one to two weeks.

FEEDING AND WATERING YOUR HORSE

WHAT YOU WILL NEED

Bucket

Fresh water

2 flakes of hay

Give the horse fresh water in a bucket. (Some horses have an automatic water dispenser that gives them water when they press their tongues to it, but this can freeze in cold climates).

Horses are born grazers and love to feed all day long. If you have a field they can graze in, terrific. If not, feed the horses twice a day. You can feed them different grasses, such as alfalfa, Bermuda, and Timothy hays. Depending on the weight of the horse, feed it at least one flake in the morning and one at night. (A flake equals 4–5 pounds of compressed hay). You can supplement a horse's diet with oats or barley, and apples and carrots also make healthy treats.

FIND A SLEDDING HILL

Behind my house, we had a sloping hill that seemed made for sledding. Tired of being housebound with two older brothers during the blizzard of '78, I piled on long underwear, a sweater, snow pants, a parka, and mittens, and made my way outside amid 40 inches of snowfall to have some prairie girl fun.

We took our orange saucers out back and gave each other running pushes to send us spinning down the track we created, from the back door, under the clothesline, and ending just as we started to enter the fallow cornfield. When I stopped, I'd run back up the hill as fast as I could plunge through the snow to sled down again.

These days, living in urban centers, I have a harder time finding appropriate places to sled. And I live in climates that don't quite generate the mounds

> **Streaked:**
> frightened or annoyed.
> *"Lily was streaked when Ned pushed her down the hill before she could settle herself properly on the sled."*

of snow necessary for a good run. Now living in the Pacific Northwest, I've scouted out a few tasty hills should we ever be blanketed with a freak snowstorm. My best friend, Alison Rooney, a New Hampshire native with a true pioneer spirit, helped me with my quest.

> **WHAT YOU WILL NEED**
> A hill with a good grade
> Sled

First, if you are familiar with the area, think about how it looks in the summer. Under that layer of pristine snow, is there a well, slough, or sinkhole you should steer clear of? If you're in the clear, make sure you avoid any obstructions, roads, or electrical lines and poles. Snow and live wires do not mix.

Find a hill with a good, lengthy grade (such as 30 percent). A steep grade could be dangerous, and a short run will cause you to be repeatedly running back up the hill. And at the bottom of your run, look for a large level area in which to end, such as a meadow. Country clubs, golf courses, and even bunny slopes at a ski resort are great places to hurl yourself down. Look for a spot near or on cross-country ski trails; the trails tend to be very hilly and sledding won't damage the trails. You could even hike up to older cemeteries as they are often not that crowded and provide good starting points for your sledding adventure. Ah, to be a homesteader with no subdivisions, highways, or telephone poles to affect your experience. Then again, you probably wouldn't be able to go sledding on Sunday afternoon, either. And that's a shame.

TIP *If you plan to sled on virgin snow, walk your course and tamp down the snow with your boots and sled. This will make your run faster and more controlled.*

PLAN A VEGETABLE GARDEN

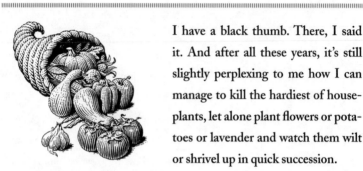 I have a black thumb. There, I said it. And after all these years, it's still slightly perplexing to me how I can manage to kill the hardiest of houseplants, let alone plant flowers or potatoes or lavender and watch them wilt or shrivel up in quick succession.

So I set out to learn all I could about planning out a vegetable garden that would not only survive but thrive. With the help of green thumbs Paul Deja and Rob Sorensen, I now feel prepared to not only eat but also grow tasty produce.

TIP   *Prune vegetables that show up early on the vine or stem, because one pepper or tomato can siphon off the plant's nutrients all for itself, leaving little for other vegetables to thrive on the plant, if they appear at all.*

Locate the sunniest part of your plot of land, and figure out how much space to allot to your garden. (Your garden should get six hours of sunlight each day.) Before thinking about what to plant, prepare your soil. I recommend creating one or several raised beds, about four feet wide, which will allow the soil to stay warmer and

WHAT YOU WILL NEED

Soil

Humus

Wood planks or large stones (optional) (the length of wood and the number of stones depends on the size of your plant bed)

Grid paper and pencil

pH test kit

Hoe

Wooden stakes

Seeds and/or seedlings

drain better. After clearing the area of weeds, grass, and moss, mound the soil about 10 inches above ground level, or enclose the raised soil in a wood frame or a border of large stones.

Mix your existing soil with humus, an organic soil component derived from decomposed plant and animal matter, and you're ready to plant your garden.

Now the fun really begins: plotting out your garden. Come up with a list of your favorite vegetables and determine the percentage of each in the garden. You probably can't plant everything, so rank your vegetables and then allot space to them accordingly.

Thinking in terms of rows, use grid paper to sketch out your tallest plants in the north part of your garden, the medium-high plants in the center, and the smaller plants in the southern end. Plant your garden in east-west rows. This configuration will ensure

Shucks:
worthless people or things (corn or pea shucks).
"The entire lot of preserves was shucks."

THE MODERN PRAIRIE GAL WAY

Since folks on the prairie lacked proper and regular refrigeration, it was difficult to keep produce throughout the winter. So our fore-mothers embraced a root cellar, a subterranean room used for storing root vegetables, butter, cream, and cured meats throughout the year. If you have a cellar or a dark, cool, humid, ventilated part of the base-ment, consider constructing a make-shift root cellar. Put up some shelves and store your hardier produce, such as potatoes, carrots, and onions, in wooden crates or bushel baskets slightly away from the wall. Remove anything that begins to spoil. This is also a great place to store canned goods, like your bread-and-butter pickles and Sweet Treat Cherries. Before long, don't be surprised to find you've amassed enough foodstuffs to see you through the most vicious of winters.

that all plants get the most sun possible and aren't overshad-owed by the tall plants (see the sidebar on the facing page for plant heights).

Know what you're planting. Consult your local nursery, the seed packet, and other garden-ers who may have experience growing a particular vegetable. If the region you live in isn't particularly kind to a particular vegetable or variety of plant (re-view a USDA Plant Hardiness Zone Map), replace that plant with an alternative more suited to your climate. Follow the speci-fications and note the expected size of the plant. Many a gar-den goes awry because seeds are planted too close together and the plants choke each other because they don't have room or sun to grow.

To ensure fresh produce from late spring through fall, include a mix of early- to late-harvest produce. While some plants can survive a late frost, wait to plant your garden until there is little chance of it.

TIP ☞ *Change the layout of your garden each year and rotate your produce. Vegetables take from and give different nutrients to the soil.*

Before planting, check the pH level of your soil. When the soil is dry, use a pH test (which you can get at a gardening center) to determine whether your soil is acidic (under 7.0) or alkaline (over 7.0). Depending on the results, you may want to mix sulfur or lime into your soil accordingly.

Use stakes to mark your rows, leaving room for you to walk. Put larger stakes in for climbing plants, such as peas, or any plants that yield heavy fruit, such as tomatoes. Make sure to label the stakes or leave markers to indicate what you plant and where. With a hoe, create a V

PLANT HEIGHTS

TALL PLANTS:

Corn

Peas

Beans

MEDIUM-HIGH PLANTS:

Tomatoes

Peppers

Pumpkins and squash

LOW-LYING PLANTS:

Carrots

Onions

Potatoes

Lettuces

down the middle of each row, matching the depth recommended for each seed. Distribute the seeds evenly down each row, adding a few extra in case some fail to germinate. Cover the seeds with soil, and pack it down firmly. Water and keep the soil moist until seedlings pop through. You are on your way to a fruitful gardening experience.

MAKE A NATURAL INSECT REPELLANT

Traditionally, my way of repelling insects has been to not go outside. Smart cookie, aren't I? I hate bug bites, always have. But I love the outdoors, so I've turned my energies toward outsmarting mosquitoes and other creepy crawlies. Out of habit, I still keep my pink bottle of calamine lotion at the ready, but happily, I don't need to actually plaster it on these days.

WHAT YOU WILL NEED

Spray bottle

¼ cup witch hazel, olive oil, rubbing alcohol, vodka, or unscented lotion

1 tablespoon citronella, cedarwood, tea tree, or sandalwood essential oil

Sterilize a spray bottle (glass or plastic) by dipping it in a pan of boiling water. Let dry. Add witch hazel and an essential oil of your choice (any of the oils listed at left are excellent mosquito repellants) to the bottle and close tightly. Shake well before each use. To use, apply liberally to any exposed areas when you are outdoors and prey to insects.

Yields: Approximately ¹/₃ cup

TIP ☞ *Forego deodorant. Many people swear that going* au natural *prevents bug bites.*

MAKE A SCARECROW

For many years, farmers have used scarecrows to prevent crows and other pesky birds from messing with their crops. Some were crude, some eerily realistic, but all were more or less effective. Growing up amidst all sorts of cornfields and apple orchards, scarecrows were a common sight. Sitting on a hay bale, surrounded by pumpkins, scarecrows became a symbol of autumn.

Here's how to make a benign but effective scarecrow. It will keep away crows and anyone who might be easily spooked.

WHAT YOU WILL NEED

One 6- to 7-foot-long
wooden stake

One 3-foot-long wooden stake

One 1-foot-long wooden stake

Hammer

Nails

Pair of neutral-colored pantyhose

Straw or hay

String

Worn shirt, pants/overalls,
and hat

Spade or shovel

Before you put your scarecrow together, you have to create a frame on which he can hang. Lay your 6-foot-long stake on the ground. About a foot from the top, lay the 3-foot-long stake perpendicularly over it and nail it firmly to the larger stake. About halfway down the long stake, nail the short stake perpendicularly as well. Your frame is ready. You just need to assemble your scarecrow.

Let's start at the top. Cut off one leg of the pantyhose and fill with straw or hay, doing your best to shape the stuffing into a ball. Place the open end over the top of the long stake and tie off the open end of the hose by wrapping string around the hose and stake.

Dress the frame by buttoning up and zipping your old clothes on the frame (slip the shirt's arms through either side of the top crossbar—which represent the shoulders—and slip the pants

Plug-ugly: rowdy or ruffian.
"The scarecrow resembled the town plug-ugly, leering from its perch at every respectable young woman who passed by."

over the bottom crossbar—the hips) and then pack tightly with hay or straw to fill out the torso, legs and arms. Tuck the shirttails into the pants so you have one packed scarecrow, not two separate parts.

To secure your scarecrow, loosen the ground with a spade or shovel. Once the end of the stake is in the ground, work it back and forth while pushing down. When it's about 1 to 1½ feet in, pack the loose dirt firmly around the scarecrow's base. Top your pantyhose head with a hat. If the hat is loose, stuff hay into the crown (it will just look like hair, adding even more authenticity to your scarecrow).

THE MODERN PRAIRIE GAL WAY

For a modern take on the traditional scarecrow, consider putting an ex-boyfriend's suit or that hideous bridesmaid's dress to good use. Follow the same directions but get creative when cleaning out your closet. I have a particularly atrocious meringue of a prom dress that could billow out in a cornfield nicely. Come to think of it, my ex-boyfriend's tattered hockey jersey would provide a colorful touch to any backyard, while also professing my team loyalty. And if you don't have any crops to guard, consider making a quirky scarecrow for your front lawn around Halloween for an unconventional addition to the neighborhood.

TIP *Place your scarecrow in the middle of your vegetable garden so that he can watch over all of your crops. Relocate the scarecrow to where the most loss is occurring. Moving him around will keep those crows on their toes.*

PREDICT THE WEATHER

In farm country, when the air went still and the birds stopped chirping, I headed for the front porch to wait. A storm was coming. The land was flat, so I had a pretty good view of gathering clouds and angry skies. And when the storm opened up over our house, I listened to the rain and soaked up the humid air from the shelter of the porch. It was exciting and comforting.

> **WHAT YOU WILL NEED**
> Patience
> Educated guesses

Predicting weather is about making educated guesses. It's hard to see what sort of weather is on its way without fancy maps, monitors, and radar, but it's hardly an exact science even with a lot of top-shelf equipment. With your female intuition and a few guiding principles, you can tell whether to bring in the laundry from the clothesline.

First, assess your geographic location and its climate. Nearby bodies of water and mountains can influence your local weather. Temperatures near the ocean are often markedly higher than they are inland because large bodies of water hold heat and warm the air. If you live on the eastern side of a mountain range, you'll experience mostly dry weather—any precipitation will fall on the western slopes before it reaches you.

Current weather conditions can help you forecast coming weather. If it's raining and the temperature is getting cooler, you can predict that the rain is going to taper off a bit. If it feels more humid and the wind is picking up a bit, take note of where it's coming from: Wind from the south/southwest is usually moist and warm, and, when combined with an incoming high wispy to low puffy cloud cover, indicates a rainstorm. Warm fronts are usually followed by a cold front, and air from the north is generally cooler and drier, so when the temperature during the storm gets cooler, the wind is probably now coming from a north or northwest direction.

A low-pressure front usually precedes a storm and a high-pressure front indicates that warmer, nice weather is on the way. To determine where areas are, stand with your back to the wind. The area of 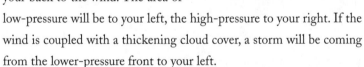 low-pressure will be to your left, the high-pressure to your right. If the wind is coupled with a thickening cloud cover, a storm will be coming from the lower-pressure front to your left.

Weather typically moves from west to east, so look westward to see what's coming your way. If a thunderstorm is developing, it will typically move from southwest to northeast. Rain comes from the northeastern section of the thunderstorm and if there was a tornado forming, it would extend from the southern edge of the cloud.

HOW THE *OLD FARMER'S ALMANAC* PREDICTS THE WEATHER

Since 1792, *The Old Farmer's Almanac* has been predicting weather, and often with surprising accuracy. The *Almanac's* founder, Robert B. Thomas, devised a super-secret formula that involved tracking sunspots. Today, the editors at the *Almanac* use solar science, climatology, and meteorology. They predict the weather by monitoring current activity both here and on the sun, and reviewing historical data and weather conditions, as well as temperature and precipitation deviations from 30-year statistical averages. But *The Old Farmer's Almanac* offers more, including planting advice, horoscopes, and tidal charts, making it a must-read for every modern prairie gal.

Watching cloud formations need not be an aimless activity. Mushroom or anvil-shaped clouds are exceptional indicators of severe weather (see cloud formations). Cumulus clouds that get bigger and taller denote instability and create precipitation.

If you're worried about frost killing your crops, know that frost is less likely as you get into spring months. Jet streams shift, bringing in warmer air from the south, as the tilt of the earth changes so that the sun is more directly overhead. If there's a frost advisory in the area, temperatures will be at or below freezing for more than four hours. Clear skies and calm winds during the day will result in an even colder night. A cloud cover blankets and holds in heat, so if the skies are clear, heat during the day will radiate away from the ground. Air has to freeze the moisture in the ground before it can lower temperatures so if the soil is dry, it's more likely that temperatures will cool off.

ARRANGE WILDFLOWERS

I've never been precious about flowers. I love wildflowers, pussy willows, cattails—basically anything you can gather on the side of the road. I'm indifferent to hothouse roses and lilies, which are lovely but lack soul. The same goes for bouquets and floral arrangements. I've never been one to mush floral putty into the bottom of a vase to get my tulips and gerbera daisies to stand at attention. I'd much rather flowers and stalks and stems droop and sway and move as they were intended in the wild. A big mess of a bouquet stuck in a Mason jar makes me happy in the most peculiar way. It reminds me of eating wild blackberries straight from the bush and picking violets in the woods while my dad was busy cutting firewood. Happy thoughts, indeed.

THE BOUQUET

WHAT YOU WILL NEED

Large Mason or Ball jar

Purified water

Wildflowers, the more varieties and colors and sizes the better

Scissors

Thoroughly clean a canning jar and fill it halfway with purified water. Estimating where the water line will be in your jar once the flowers are added, remove leaves and excess foliage, which decay quickly and will foul up your water.

Place your wildflowers in a sink filled with cold water. While a stem is submerged, cut it at a slant. If the stem is thick, crush it a bit,

THE MODERN PRAIRIE GAL WAY

Hostess gifts have gotten more and more elaborate since pioneer times, but I've always found the most appreciated gifts to be ones that come from the heart, not necessarily Cartier. I like to give a batch of cookies, a book I loved that I want to share, or a bundle of wildflowers tied with a ribbon. Or tell them how much you adore their children by making garlands (18 inches for them) for each of them. You can bet you'll be invited back.

which will help hydrate the stem and bloom.

Cut your stems to different heights so the blooms won't compete for space once in the jar. Start by placing one large bloom in your jar at a slant. On the opposite side of the jar, place another bloom of equal size and/or color. Do this all the way around the jar, first using larger and taller stalks and then filling in holes with more delicate and shorter stems. The goal is not perfection and symmetry but rather a vibrant explosion of color, shape, and texture.

If you want to change the water, do not expose your stems to air. Instead, place your jar in a sink and pour fresh water (preferably purified) into the jar until the water overflows and runs clear.

The Wildflower Crown

Remove the leaves and thorns from the stems. Trim the stems so they are all roughly 3 inches long.

WHAT YOU WILL NEED

Approximately
50 wildflowers with stems on
(the number you need depends
on the size of the bloom; the larger
the flower, the less you need)

String or wire (optional)

4–6 bobby pins (optional)

Lay three flowers side by side on a table, with the stems pointing toward you. You are basically going to braid the stems together. To do this, lay the right stem over the center stem so that the end of it becomes the center stem. Now lay the left stem over the center stem so that becomes the middle stem.

Add a new stem to the right side and, holding on to that and the other right stem (the stem immediately next to it), lay them both over the center stem. Add a stem to the left now and hold it with the other left stem (the stem immediately next to it), laying it across the center stem. If it becomes difficult to hold on to your two right or left stems as you braid, twist them gently a couple of times to join them before braiding.

Continue in this manner until your braided garland measures 22 to 23 inches in length. Weave the stem end of your garland around the beginning bloom end by tucking each stem through holes in your braid. If you like, tie the ends together with string or wire for added security.

Place your masterpiece on the crown of your head. If necessary, secure with bobby pins. You're a prairie princess!

SQUARE DANCE

While dancing at a dark club to remixed pop songs has its place, nothing can replace the exhilaration of vigorous country dancing. Square dancing as we know it started out as European country dances. As American settlers moved west and spread out, it became necessary for a figure caller to help dancers maneuver through the steps.

If you've got the space, clear out the barn, room, or field, and host a proper square dance for a group of your friends (at least four couples). Invite them over and encourage swishy skirts, cowboy boots, and belt buckles, the bigger the better. While you're going for prairie, it's okay if a few veer into cowboy territory.

For fun, practice one song and play caller (you know, the one that says, "Grab your partner, do-si-do"). As guests arrive, hand them an instruction sheet. Lead a short tutorial by taking them through a few basic steps and combinations.

You could even put footsteps on the ground to help dancers maneuver through a move. A little research should allow you to put together a mix of music appropriate for actual square dances along with music for guests to dance freely and without direction. After all, you want to enjoy yourself at your own party.

Keep the decorations simple. Place buckets of wildflowers around the room, well out of dancers' way. Spread gingham over tables, and serve ice-cold lemonade, root beer floats, and veggie platters fresh from your garden. Send guests home with a small bottle of foot lotion or a CD of fiddle music.

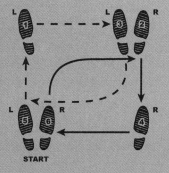

HONARARY PRAIRIE GALS AND GUYS

This book could not have happened without the generous assistance of many crafty and knowledgeable folks. I am forever indebted to the following people, some of whom I've had the pleasure of sitting down with and others with whom I look forward to shooting the breeze, perhaps over a pot of tea or a slice of rhubarb pie.

MARY ANNE AIELLO, Director of Chickadee Music in Seattle, shares the joy of music with families of infants, toddlers, and preschoolers through the Music Together® program.

Native Michigander JOEL BLAKEMAN got his passion for baking and cooking from his Hungarian grandmother and his grandparents' blueberry farm. His expertise lies in baking and soup-making. He currently lives in Tampa, Florida.

CYNTHIA CECHOTA enjoys preparing traditional, nutrient-dense foods for friends and family. She resides part-time in a tiny cabin with an old-fashioned composting (sawdust) privy.

CHEF GABRIEL CLAYCAMP, a graduate of the Culinary Institute of America, is the owner of Culinary Communion, a small cooking school in Seattle specializing in intimate hands-on culinary education. Gabriel's passion is charcuterie, at last count making 38 different cured meats out of his home.

A medical technologist raising three children in Upstate New York, PERI COLEMAN has lived on a sheep farm, counted pollen for Albany County, and enjoys making home-cooked meals and treats for her family and friends.

The author's stepsister AMY CRISENBERY is an office manager. She lives in the Ann Arbor, Michigan area with her husband and two kids.

PAUL DEJA lives in Southwestern Michigan, where tending to the family farm has always been a part of his life.

The author's mother JUDY ECKELBARGER grew up in Southwestern Michigan, learning to can bushels of "everything" from her mother. Today, she puts up bread-and-butter pickles, tomatoes, and beets, and freezes corn, string beans, and strawberry jam. An antique dealer for many years, she has carved and painted decoy ducks, and dabbled in decoupage, ceramics, and toll painting.

The author's stepfather JIM ECKELBARGER grew up on a Michigan farm learning how to raise and slaughter chickens, hunt, fish, cut wood, and grow and sell corn. He watched his dad make cherries ever since he could remember, and as a boy, he'd sneak one now and then when his dad wasn't looking

Although graphic designer, illustrator, and teacher LIDA ENCHE-KEENE resides in Seattle, she pines for the big open skies, June bugs, flying cockroaches, fire ants, lightning storms, and sweet-grass smell of her childhood in Southeastern Texas.

ALICIA FREILE is a Philadelphia-based designer and the owner of Gauchita, a T-shirt and handbag label featuring her original embroidery designs.

A *Little House* fan, BARBARA FREILE is a third-grade teacher in Lancaster, Pennsylvania, whose mother was raised on a farm during the Depression. She teaches a reading unit on *Sarah Plain & Tall* each year.

ELISE BALLARD GILBERT lives, cooks, and works as a marketing consultant in Seattle, Washington.

The author's uncle, GREG HAMLIN, is an automation engineer in Saint Paul, Minnesota. He's been whittling and carving since he was a Boy Scout in the early 1960s.

Philadelphia, Pennsylvania psychic VIVIENNE McCARTHY learned to brew tea growing up in Ireland, where black Indian tea is the most coveted. Her grandmom used to say that, "A cup of tea is acknowledged to be the greatest of all restoratives." Her career has been based on the reading of the tea leaves, which she believes can change destinies.

Seattle mom and all-around prairie gal CAMILLE MILLER is an expert in cranberry and popcorn garlands because she's thrifty and couldn't find anything at the mercantile that looked like strung cranberries.

PAULA NASIATKA has been riding horses for more than 20 years. She lives with her husband, daughter, horse, and dog next to Saguaro National Park in Tucson, Arizona.

ALISON ROONEY is a communications consultant serving cultural, medical, educational, legal, publishing, and nonprofit clients. A New England native and sledding pro, she now lives in Philadelphia.

Mixed-media artist and cowgirl at heart WENDY SLONEKER currently lives and loves in Seattle with her dachshund Otto.

Edmonton, Alberta, native ROB SORENSEN may live in Seattle now, but he knows all about living in a harsh climate and shared his expertise on ice fishing and planning a garden.

Seattle meteorologist REBECCA STEVENSON holds the Seal of Approval from both the American Meteorological Society and the National Weather Association.

SUSIE STEVENSON is a member of Southern Comforters Quilt Guild in Bowie, Maryland. Her most prized possessions are two antique quilts made by her great-great grandmother in 1843 and 1880. She always thought that she was born 100 years too late and would have made a terrific prairie girl.

MELISSA WAGNER is the co-author of *Field Guide to Stains: How to Identify and Remove Virtually Every Stain Known to Man* (www.quirkbooks.com), the funniest guide to stain removal currently on the market. She lives in Philadelphia.

GINA WILDE, knitwear designer and motor of Alchemy Yarns (www.alchemyyarns.com), lives and hand-paints luxury natural fiber on a farm north of San Francisco.

The author's brother, CHRIS WORICK, is a retired soldier who has always loved history and exploring his surroundings in search of historical artifacts. An amateur gold panner, he currently lives Dahlonega, Georgia, site of the nation's first true gold rush.

The author's sister-in-law MONIKA WORICK grew up on a small farm in the Black Forest region of Germany where her family grew potatoes, wheat, and animal-feed, kept livestock, tended a large garden and fruit trees, and basically lived off the land.

The author's dad, WILLIS WORICK, is the son of a fruit farmer. He grew up in rural Southwestern Michigan during the 1940s and '50s, when they had animals and used them for eggs, milk, meat, and working in the fields; went barefoot all summer; and labored in the fields from early spring to late fall.

DAWN ZELIGMAN is a former suburban dweller turned country bumpkin who balances life in Michigan as a graduate student, college administrator, farmer, and avid colonial craftsperson.

INDEX